MW01622898

Life of Fred®

Australia

Life of Fred®
Australia

Stanley F. Schmidt, Ph.D.

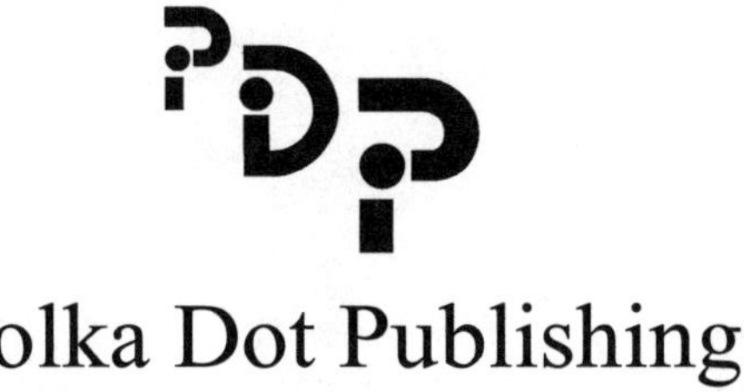

Polka Dot Publishing

ISBN: 978-1-937032-12-8

Printed and bound in the United States of America

Polka Dot Publishing Reno, Nevada

To order copies of books in the Life of Fred series,

visit our website PolkaDotPublishing.com

Questions or comments? Email the author at lifeoffred@yahoo.com

Third printing

for Goodness' sake

or as J.S. Bach—who was
never noted for his plain
English—often expressed it:

Ad Majorem Dei Gloriam

(to the greater glory of God)

If you happen to spot an error that the author, the publisher, and the printer missed, please let us know with an email to: lifeoffred@yahoo.com

SPECIAL OFFER

As a reward, we'll email back to you a list of all the corrections that readers have reported.

A Note Before We Begin

This is the first language arts book in the Life of Fred® series. In these language arts books, we will cover English from every angle.

This first book will cover a zillion topics including:

✯ the right way to hold a pencil
✯ postscripts in letters
✯ eight ways to make plurals in English
✯ the 14 punctuation marks
✯ silent letters
✯ homonyms (a.k.a. homophones)
✯ hyperbole
✯ when to use *that* and when to use *which*

This is only a partial list.

For maximum happiness, let's not begin this book too early.

There are other things that need to be done before studying heteronyms.

HOW THIS BOOK IS ORGANIZED

Each chapter is a daily lesson consisting of about four pages of the adventures of Fred and a Your Turn to Play.

Have a paper and pencil handy before you sit down to read.

Each Your Turn to Play consists of about three or four questions. Write out the answers—don't just orally answer them.

After all the questions are answered, then take a peek at my answers that are given on the next page.

Don't just read the questions and look at the answers. You won't learn as much that way.

A NOTE FROM STAN

The government schools and most textbooks practice a form of segregation. In the English class they study only English. In the math class they study only math. In history, only history. In geography, only geography.

I believe there is an inner coherence among all the subjects. I do not teach English. I teach kids. In some of the Life of Fred math books there is piano sheet music. In this book I include the geography of the oceans, the capital of Kansas, the four ways to try to figure out what a continent is,* and what to do if you are lost in an airport.

I believe in play, in having fun. Most textbooks are boring and dry. Who picks up a textbook to read in their leisure time? I have tried to write the wettest books I can!

Stan

---

* A continent isn't just a big piece of land separated from other big pieces of land by water. Asia and Europe are different continents but are not separated by water.

Contents

Chapter One
The World

Fred was excited. It was Sunday morning and time to go to Sunday school. He brushed his teeth, put on a clean shirt, and ran to the chapel on the KITTENS University campus.

On Monday, Tuesday, Wednesday, Thursday, and Friday, Fred teaches math at the university. On Sunday he gets to be a student.

He likes to teach, and he likes to be a student. Both are fun. Fred is five years old.

Fred was the first student to arrive. It was ten minutes to nine. Class started at nine o'clock. Fred liked to be early so that he could help Carrie set up the tables and chairs.

8:50 a.m.

Carrie

Carrie taught Sunday School for the five-year-olds. She was a very popular teacher. All the kids had a good time in her class.

Carrie put up four tables and Fred put seven chairs at each table. That made space for 28 students. Fred knew that four times seven is equal to 28. He knew more math than most five-year-olds.

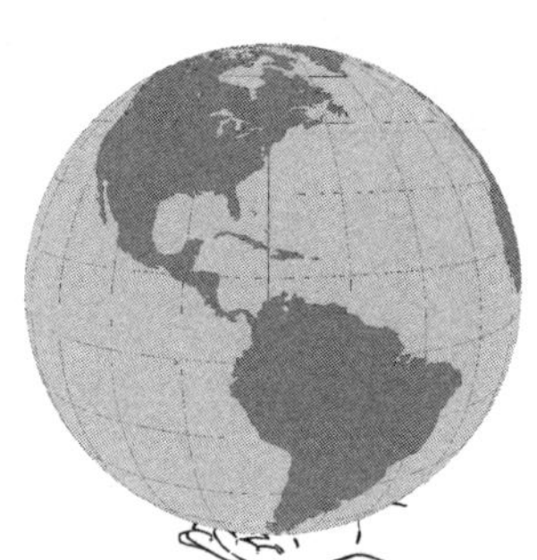

By nine o'clock all the chairs were filled. Carrie said, "Today we are going to look at something really big."

Kelly raised her hand. "That's not so big. It is only one foot tall."

Carrie explained, "This ball is the whole world. About seven billion* people live here."

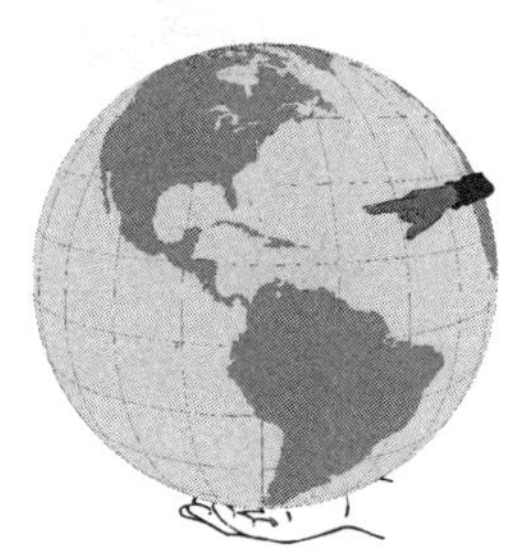

Percy shouted, "I bet nobody is living here." He pointed to the middle of the Atlantic Ocean.

Kelly disagreed. "Somebody could be on a boat out there."

Carrie continued, "No matter where people live, we are to do good things for all of them."

Percy shouted, "All seven billion of them?"

---

* Seven billion = 7,000,000,000 (nine zeros)

Kelly raised her hand and said, "Maybe seven billion and one if someone just had a baby."

Fred thought about the day that he was born. Most people can't remember the day that they were born. Fred has a very good memory.

Percy asked, "Is it snack time yet?" It was five minutes after nine.

Carrie told the class that it was time for the arts and crafts part of Sunday School.

> Time Out!
>
> Fred had trouble getting used to Sunday School for five-year-olds. Carrie held up a globe of the world and told the children that they were to do good things for everyone on earth. That was the end of her talk.
>
> When Fred lectured to college students at KITTENS University, he talked for 50 minutes.
>
> These five-year-olds couldn't pay attention for even five minutes.

Kelly raised her hand and asked, "Can I help?"

Carrie let her pass out the crayons. Then she asked the class, "Is there anyone who would like to pass out the coloring sheets?"

Percy shouted, "Me!"

Fred wondered why Percy was always shouting.

Here is the sheet that Percy tossed in front of each student:

Fred was very good at math, but he wasn't very good at coloring. This is the best that he could do:

Fred needed coloring lessons!

Fred wasn't very good at art either. The mosquito that he drew doesn't look like the ones on the coloring sheet.

This is your first Your Turn to Play. It deals with beginnings and endings.

To begin, please take out a piece of paper. Write down your answers before you turn the page and look at my answers. (To answer the first question you will write down either 1. A or 1. B or 1. C.)

Your Turn to Play

1. There are three paragraphs at the top of this page. How do you begin a paragraph?

A. You draw a cat to start a paragraph.

B. You make about five spaces and then start the first sentence.

C. You yell, "New paragraph coming!"

2. There are three ways to end a sentence.

A. You write a period (.) or a question mark (?) or an exclamation mark (!).

B. You yell, "I'm ending my sentence right now!"

C. You draw a dancing dog.

. . . . ANSWERS . . . .

1. The correct answer is *B. You make about five spaces and then start the first sentence.*

Those spaces are called an **indentation**. (four syllables!)

If you use a ruler, you can check that each indentation in this book is one-half inch long. One way to make an indentation is to hit the Tab → key.

2. The correct answer is *A. You write a period (.) or a question mark (?) or an exclamation mark (!).*

Imagine a world in which there were no periods, question marks, or exclamation marks to end sentences—and no capital letters to begin sentences.*

i would hate to try to read in such a world everything would be jammed together with no periods it would be hard to tell when a sentence ended with no capital letters it would be more difficult to tell the start of a new sentence

---

* Actually, punctuation in the English language did not come into common use until the invention of the printing press (about 1450).

Chapter Two
Questions

Kelly looked at Fred's drawing. She pointed to . "That's a funny horse. Its tail is too big."

Fred was embarrassed. He looked at her coloring sheet. The mosquito she had drawn was beautiful. It really looked like a mosquito.

He turned his paper over so that no one could see his drawing. He took a pencil out of his pocket and did a little math.

$2^3 = 2 \times 2 \times 2 = 8$

This coloring sheet brought to you by . . .

Board of Missions, 123 Main Street, Reno, Nevada 89521

Please write to us.

Kelly looked at Fred's math and said, "You are supposed to write your numbers all the same size. Your 3 is too small."

Fred was going to explain to her that he wasn't trying to write 23, but 2^3, which is two to the third power. That was something from algebra.

Before he could say a word, she raised her hand and told the teacher that she was bored.

Percy shouted, "I'm done!" He had folded his coloring sheet into a paper airplane and sent it flying toward the trash basket. It missed.

Carrie knew it was time for her class to do something else. She said, "Let's play the Good Shepherd game."

Everyone ran to the costume box and dressed up as lambs.

Kelly got the perfect lamb outfit. Fred put his coloring paper in his pocket and then headed to the costume box. Everyone else had already picked out the good lamb outfits.

Fred did the best that he could.

Fred with rabbit ears

As the old saying goes, "*The early bird gets the worm.*" This means that if there is a limited amount of something, don't be late.

After each child got to be a "precious little lamb" (or in Fred's case, a "precious little rabbit"), game time was over.

Carrie told her class that for the next five minutes it was free play time. "Are there any questions?"

Percy shouted, "When is snack time?"

Kelly raised her hand and asked, "Who can I play with?"

Percy shouted, "How can I survive without a snack?"

Kelly asked Percy, "Why are you always thinking about food?"

Percy looked around and asked, "Food? Did somebody mention food? Where is it?"

Fred took off his rabbit ears and put them back into the costume box. He giggled to himself and thought, *Percy and Kelly have used all five of the famous question words: when, who, how, why, and where.*

I wish the question words were five W's. That would be prettier. English is messier than math. That's why I like teaching math. Two plus two equals four on every day of the week.

> Time Out for Older Readers!
>
> Fred thought, "I wish the question words were five w's." He didn't think, "I wish the question words was five w's."
>
> He was using the subjunctive mood to indicate something that was currently not true. If I were writing in German, French, or Latin, I would use the subjunctive mood much more frequently. In English the use of the subjunctive is dying out.

Carrie had given her class five minutes of free play time so that she could go in the other room and get the milk and cookies ready for their snack time.

The 28 students did lots of different things.

✔ Four of them played hopscotch.

✔ Ten of them played tag.

✔ One of them (Kelly) helped clean up the room. Some of the kids had thrown their lamb costumes on the floor. She picked them up and put them in the costume box.

✔ Nine of them sat and talked with their friends.

✔ Two of them put their heads on the table and shut their eyes. They had stayed up late on Saturday night watching television. They were tired.

4	hopscotch
10	tag
1	clean up
9	talk
+ 2	nap
26	

There were 28 students. Twenty-six of them were doing things that normal five-year-olds do. Two students (Percy and Fred) were doing things that most five-year-old do not do.

✔ Percy picked up some chairs and put them on top of the table. When Kelly asked him what he was doing, he said that he was building a mountain.

Then he climbed up to the top of his mountain.

Please take out a piece of paper and write your answers before you look at my answers.

Your Turn to Play

1. Draw a picture of Percy at the top of his mountain of chairs.

2. It is fun to make up questions using the five question words: when, who, how, why, and where.

For example:

When did Percy make his mountain?

Who might get hurt during the free play time?

Where did Carrie go?

Now it's your turn. Make up a question using either *why* or *how*.

3. If you stay up really late on Saturday night, on which day will you be tired?

.......ANSWERS.......

1. Here is the picture that Fred drew. Your picture will probably look different from his.

2. Writing a question can be hard until you get used to it. Once you have done it, it starts to get easier.

Here are some possible questions using *why* and *how*:

Why did Percy build the mountain of chairs?

Why did Carrie leave the room?

How did Percy climb on top of the chairs?

How will Percy get down?

Why didn't someone run and tell Carrie what he was doing?

How high was the mountain?

Why does Percy shout all the time?

3. The day that follows Saturday is Sunday. If you stay up late on Saturday night, you will probably be tired on Sunday.

Chapter Three
Letter Writing

Crash! Percy's mountain of chairs collapsed. He fell on the carpet. Luckily, none of the chairs fell on top of him.

Carrie rushed into the room to see what had happened.

Percy stood up and said, "Everything's okay." Percy didn't shout his words. He was a little worried that he had gotten into trouble.

Carrie said, "As long as you weren't hurt, it's all right*."

Fred had been sitting at the table next to Percy's mountain of chairs writing a letter.

Fred was now lying on the floor. All the chairs had fallen on top of him.

"Where is Fred?" Carrie asked.

No one knew.

---

* There is no such word as *alright.*

Kelly raised her hand and said, "Fred must have been here. I see the paper he was writing on."

Carrie picked up the paper and read it:

June 2

Dear Friends at the Board of Missions,

On the coloring sheet you wrote, "Please write to us" I am writing to you.

I want to be a friend, help people in trouble, teach, dig a well to get clean water, and kill mosquitos.

I don't know how to dig a well or kill mosquitos, but I do love to teach. I have been teaching at KITTENS University for five years.

With my best wishes,

Fred Gauss

P.S. My last name rhymes with house

The chairs must have hit Fred just as he was writing the last word in his letter. He didn't get a chance to put a period at the end of the sentence.

Some notes about the letter:

♪#1: Fred forgot to put a year in the date at the top of the letter.

♪#2: Since it was early June, the spring semester at KITTENS University was over. Fred was looking forward to summer vacation. He was looking forward to doing some good things for other people.*

♪#3: "P.S." means **postscript**. A postscript is a part of the letter after it has been signed by the writer. Most letters do not have postscripts.

Fred wrote his postscript because many people think that Fred Gauss is pronounced Fred Goose or Fred Gauze. Someone once even called him Fred Gas.

Fred used to tell his students that Gauss rhymes with mouse. One of his students (Joe) drew on his paper:

Fred changed it to, "rhymes with house."

---

* Fred was not like some five-year-olds who spend their summers watching television, eating ice cream, and asking their mothers, "What shall I do?"

Postscript can be written as either P.S. or p.s. Both are correct.

Ps. = Psalm
ps = picosecond (one trillionth of a second = $\frac{1}{1,000,000,000,000}$ seconds.*)
ps. = pieces

Carrie thought that Fred's letter was beautiful and decided that the Board of Missions should see what one of her five-year-old students was thinking.

She addressed an envelope, put Fred's letter in it, and dropped it in the campus mailbox in her room.

Kelly raised her hand and said, "I think I know where Fred is." She had heard Oooooooooo coming from underneath the pile of chairs. It was Fred. He was moaning.

Everyone helped unpile the chairs. Fred was sitting on the floor with a big bump on his head. That was his only injury. He was still holding his pencil.

---

* When your mother calls you, you can say, "I'll be there in a picosecond."

Fred said, "I guess I shouldn't have been sitting so close to that dangerous pile of chairs. As the old saying goes, '*Better safe than sorry.*' "

Your Turn to Play

1. On your paper draw a big rectangle. We will pretend it is an envelope. Show how you would write the address Board of Missions, 123 Main Street, Reno, Nevada 89521 and show where you would put the stamp.

2. Which of these is the best example of *Better safe than sorry*?

A. Eating a peanut-butter-and-jelly sandwich.

B. Wearing your seat belt when you are in a car.

C. Playing the piano.

3. Fred was wrong when he thought there were five famous question words: When, Who, How, Why, and Where—four W's and one H. There are six famous question words.

What do you think is the sixth one?

. . . . ANSWERS . . . .

1. Your paper should look something like this:

Board of Missions
123 Main Street
Reno, Nevada 89521

Please note: (1) The post office prefers you use the state abbreviations when addressing envelopes. In this case it would be Reno, NV 89521. (2) I am not sure what kind of bird is on that stamp. (3) There is no Board of Missions at 123 Main Street. That is just part of the story. In fact, there is no Main Street in Reno.

2. The answer is B. Wearing your seat belt when you are in a car.

The reason you wear a seat belt in a car is to protect you in case of an accident.

The reason you brush your teeth is so that your teeth stay healthy. You will be sorry if the dentist finds holes in your teeth.

The reason you swim where there is a lifeguard is so that you remain safe.

The reason you wear rain clothes or take an umbrella when it looks cloudy is so that you don't end up wet and sorry.

The reason you don't sit right next to someone who is piling chairs up into a mountain is so that you don't get a bump on your head.

3. **What** is the sixth famous question word.

When people are learning to be reporters for newspaper or television, they are told to write their story using who, what, when, where, why, and how.

Example: This morning (when), Fred Gauss (who) got a bump on his head (what) in Sunday School (where) when some chairs fell on him (how) because he was sitting too close to Percy (why).

Chapter Four
Snack Time

Fred knew the correct way to hold a pencil. You use the first three fingers. Your ring finger and your pinky do not touch the pencil.

correct way to hold a pencil

incorrect way
to hold a pencil

Fred put his pencil down and rubbed his head.

Percy said, “I’m sorry.”

Fred accepted Percy’s apology, “It’s okay. Accidents will happen.”

Carrie announced that it was snack time.

Percy was the first one to get a chair and sit at a table. He yelled, “I’m starved!”

The other 27 students got their chairs and sat quietly.

“Who will help pass out the cookies?” Carrie asked.

Kelly raised her hand.

"Who will help pass out the milk?" Carrie asked.

Percy did not offer to help. He figured that if he helped, then he would not be the first one to be eating and drinking.

Fred helped with the milk.

There were 28 cookies and 28 kids. Each kid got a cookie. Fred put his cookie in his pocket. He wasn't very hungry.

Percy wanted to show off. He took his cookie and broke it in half. He held up

the two halves and shouted, "I have twice as many cookies as anyone else."

Not all five-year-olds are alike.

⇛ Most of the other students ignored Percy.

⇛ Four of the students broke their cookies in half.

⇛ One boy broke his cookie into a million pieces and said, "I've got more cookies than anyone else."

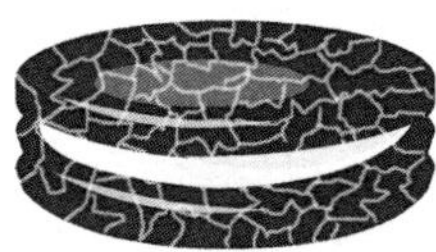

⇛ Fred was good at math. He thought, *Percy is silly. One half plus one half is equal to two halves. And two halves is the same as one regular cookie. Percy has more pieces but only one cookie.*

In English you write one half plus one half is equal to one. In math you write $\frac{1}{2} + \frac{1}{2} = 1$. Fred liked math better because it was shorter.

He might have been prejudiced in favor of math because he taught mathematics at KITTENS University. He didn't realize that he had to use English in order to teach math!

But Fred was glad that he didn't have to teach English. English was messier than math.

Fred's favorite example of messy English was in making **plurals** of words.

You start with one dog. The plural is dogs.

That is nice. You just add an *s*.

one cat → two cats
one pizza → two pizzas
one cow → two cows
one house → two houses
one car → two cars

But if the word ends in *f* then the plural is *ves*.

one half → two halves
one calf → two calves
 one wolf → two wolves 

If that were all there was to making plurals in English, it wouldn't be so bad. The rule could be: *To make a plural, add an* s. *If the word ends in* f, *then change the* f *to* ves. But that rule doesn't always work.

The plural of roof is roofs.

Fred handed out a straw with each carton of milk.

You can guess what Percy did. He tore his straw in half, held up the two pieces, and shouted, "I've got twice as many straws as anyone else."

⇛ Almost everyone ignored Percy. They were tired of his showing off.

⇛ One boy tore his straw into a million pieces and said, "I've got more straws than anyone else." His straws were so short that they couldn't be used to suck up the milk. He had to throw his pieces into the trash.

⇛ Fred wasn't very thirsty. He put his carton of milk into his pocket next to the cookie. (He had large pockets.)

Your Turn to Play

Let's do some plurals . . .

1. Fill in the word: one rabbit → two __________

   one ant → two __________

   one frog → two __________

2. Fill in the word: one elf → two __________

   one hoof → two __________

Here are some really weird plurals . . .

3. Fill in the word: one child → two __________

   one tooth → two __________

   one foot → two __________

Children have 20 baby teeth. Half (10) of them are in the upper jaw and half (10) are in the lower jaw.

The first baby teeth usually appear when the baby is six to twelve months old. The last ones appear before the age of three.

Adults get 32 adult teeth. How many they keep depends in part on doing a good job of flossing and brushing.

.......ANSWERS.......

1. one rabbit → two rabbits
   one ant → two ants
   one frog → two frogs

2. one elf → two elves
   one hoof → two hooves*

3. one child → two children
   one tooth → two teeth
   one foot → two feet

There are zillions of **irregular plurals** in English. (goose → geese, mouse → mice, self → selves) A regular plural is any plural in which you just add an *s*.

Fred's favorite irregular plurals are:

one sheep → two sheep

one moose → two moose.

He would be really happy if all plurals were this easy.

---

* The plural of *hoof* can also be *hoofs*. Both *hooves* and *hoofs* are correct.

Chapter Five
The Call

It was 10 o'clock. The church service was over and the parents came to pick up their kids from Sunday school.

When Kelly's parents came, she jumped into her father's arms. She didn't raise her hand, because she wasn't in class anymore.

When Percy's dad came, he shouted, "How did it go, son?"

Percy shouted back, "Just great!" He didn't mention the mountain of chairs he had built.

No one picked up Fred.* He walked out of the university chapel, passed the tennis courts, through the rose gardens, and to the Math Building. He climbed two flights of stairs and walked down the hallway past nine vending machines to room 314. This is where he lived.

---

* The story of how Fred and his doll, Kingie, faced the world alone when he was six months old is told in *Life of Fred: Calculus.* Calculus is studied in the first two years of college.

He walked in. His doll was busy finishing up an oil painting. Kingie's art was much better than Fred's.

Kingie

Kingie's
"The Sea Bird"

Fred's
"See the Bird"

Every person has things that they do best. Fred liked to do math. Kingie liked to do oil painting.

When you are just a baby, there isn't much you can do.

- ➢ Smiling is good.
- ➢ Kelly raised her hand a lot.
- ➢ Percy screamed.
- ➢ Fred was doing math in his head.

As you grow up you discover more and more things about yourself.

- ➢ I'm good at ice hockey.
- ➢ I like learning Latin.
- ➢ I like babies.
- ➢ I enjoy office work.

- ➢ I love nineteenth century English poetry.
- ➢ I want to open a pizza restaurant.
- ➢ I want to work in a zoo.
- ➢ I want to work at an abattoir. (AB-eh-twa)
- ➢ I want to sing opera.
- ➢ I really like cooking carrots.

Everyone is different. Sometimes it takes a half of a lifetime to figure out your calling.

Fred's calling sat on his desk. It was a large envelope. He opened it.

Board of Missions
123 Main Street
Reno NV 89521

June 2, 2013

Dear Mr. Gauss,

We were holding our board meeting when your letter arrived. We were looking for someone just like you for work in Australia.

You wrote to us that you love teaching, and we have a great need for an experienced teacher such as you for the summer.

If interested, please let us know and report to our office in Wagga Wagga on June 4.

Sincerely,

Jennifer Glory

Jennifer Glory
Board chairman

Fred was overjoyed. It was a chance to "do good things" for the people of the world, which is what Carrie had said in Sunday school.

It was an opportunity to go to Australia.

It was a chance to teach math.

Fred dashed off a reply:

Dear Jennifer,

Yes!

With great expectations,

Fred

Fred ran down the hallway past the nine vending machines (four on the left and five on the right) and put his letter in the mailbox.

Time Out!

There are a lot of things that need to be explained.

First of all, Carrie had put Fred's first letter in the campus mailbox during Sunday school. Fred received a reply on his desk by the time he had walked from the university chapel to his office. How was this possible? This was Sunday. Fred's letter went from Kansas to Reno. The board's letter went from Reno to Kansas.

Answer: KITTENS campus mail is a little different than ordinary mail. There are mailboxes almost everywhere. You are never more than 50 yards from a mailbox. KITTENS campus mail is fast. Whenever any mail is deposited in a box, a special light on the top turns on. Student letter carriers rush over to the box and get the mail and run to deliver it. It's faster than email.

Second, Fred had written that he had been teaching at the university for five years, but he didn't mention how old he was.

Third, did Fred mention in his letter that he taught math? The answer is a two-letter word beginning with the letter n.

Your Turn to Play

1. The **opening salutation** of a letter begins with the word `Dear`.

These are **punctuation marks**:

. , ! ? ; : " " — ' ( ) [ ]

period, comma, exclamation mark, question mark, semicolon, colon, quotation marks, dash, apostrophe, parentheses, brackets

Which punctuation mark goes at the end of an opening salutation? (If you don't know, look back in this book to any of the three letters.)

2. At the end of a letter, just before the signature, is the **closing salutation**. There are a zillion possible closing salutations.

Which punctuation mark goes at the end of a closing salutation?

.......ANSWERS.......

1. Most of the time, a comma is used at the end of an opening salutation.

Dear Fred,

Dear Mr. Gauss,

Dear President Taft,

An opening salutation is never indented. This paragraph is indented.

2. The closing salutation ends with a comma.

If you indent your paragraphs, begin the closing salutation at the center.

Yours truly,

or Sincerely,

or Love and kisses,

or With my best wishes,

Only the first word in a closing salutation is capitalized.

In a formal or business letter, the opening salutation often ends with a colon.

Dear Sir or Madam:

You are hereby drafted into the United States Army. Report for duty at 7 a.m.

Chapter Six
Geography

Today was June 2, and Fred needed to be in Australia by June 4. He had two days to get there.

He told Kingie, "I'm going to Australia!"

"Do you know where that is?" Kingie asked.

Fred didn't know. He took out his book of maps—called an atlas—and looked at a map of Kansas.

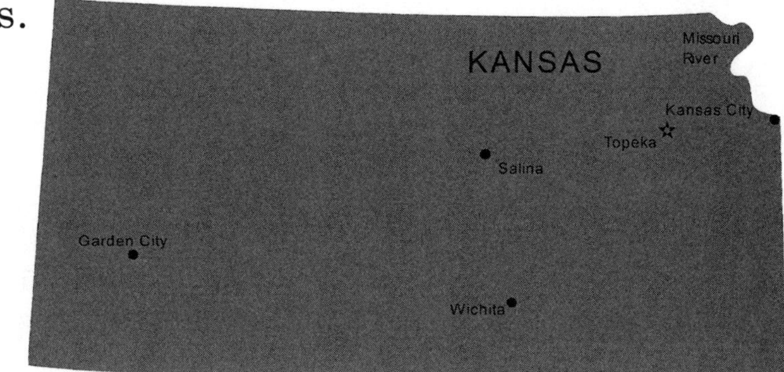

It wasn't a very good map. It only showed five cities and one river. Looking at the map he knew that Topeka was the capital of the state. It was marked with a star.

Fred said, "I can't find Australia on the map."

Kingie stopped painting and looked at the map. He told Fred, "Australia isn't in Kansas. You are looking at the wrong map."

Fred got out a map of the United States.*

Fred looked and looked. He couldn't find Australia.

Kingie couldn't believe what he was seeing. Fred was excited about going to Australia, and he didn't have any idea where Australia was. He told Fred, "You are looking between the Pacific and Atlantic oceans. Those are the wrong two oceans. Australia is between the Indian and the Pacific oceans."

"But I don't see any Indian Ocean on the map," Fred said.

---

* Do you live in one of these states? This is a map of the 48 contiguous (con-TIG-you-us) states. *Contiguous* means two different things: either touching or being close without touching. If I stand close to you, we are contiguous. If we hold hands, we are contiguous.

"That's because you have the wrong map! The Indian ocean is not contiguous with the United States. Get out a world map."

Fred turned to a world map in his atlas.

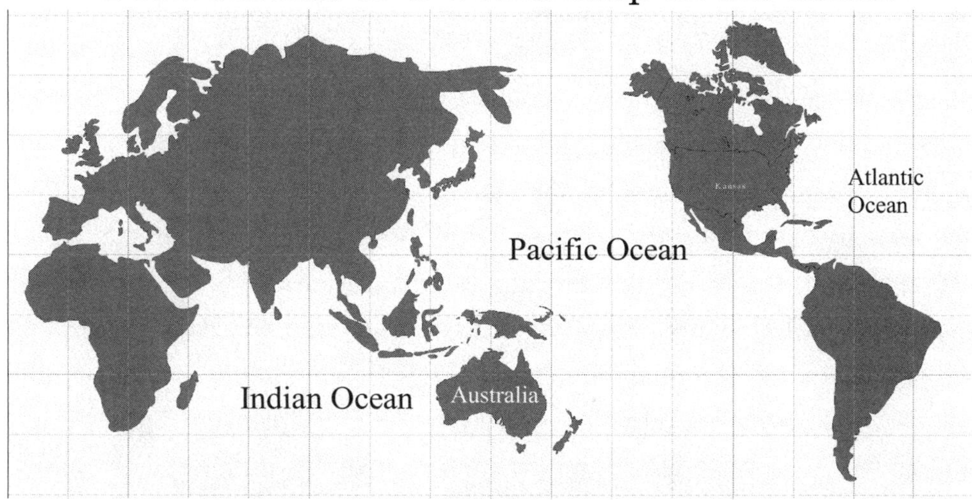

All kinds of thoughts went through Fred's head:

❀ Most of the world is ocean.

❀ Every person lives somewhere on this map.

❀ Australia is almost as large as the United States.

❀ I won't be able to take a bus to get from Kansas to Australia. Buses can't float.

Fred was learning geography.*

---

* (jee-OG-graf-ee) Geography = where things are on a map. It also is the study of climate (rainy, dry, hot, cold, windy), population, and land use (cities, farms, highways, and pizza restaurant locations).

"I found Australia," Fred told Kingie. It looks like a giant island.*

Kingie went back to painting. He didn't want to try and explain the difference between an **island** and a **continent** to Fred.

small essay

The Big Island-Continent Fight

In most geography classes in elementary schools, the students are taught that there are seven continents: North America, South America, Asia, Europe, Africa, Australia, and Antarctica.

The students who memorize this list might get a gold star or an A on their report card.

A student who is thinking might ask, "What's a continent?" That is a really good question to ask when you are supposed to memorize that list of continents.

Some teachers might not know the answer. They might say, "The world is divided into seven continents," but that doesn't explain what a continent is.

They might point to the seven continents on the map, but that doesn't define what a continent is.

---

* The *s* in *island* is silent. It's called a **silent letter**.
The *k* in *knife* is silent. The *b* in *comb* is silent.

Some geography teachers might not be able to give the definition of a continent. That's not because they are dumb. (There is a silent *b* in *dumb*). It is because there is no definition that everyone agrees on.

Math is different. Everyone agrees that a rhombus (ROM-bus, it has a silent *h*) is a flat four-sided figure in which all four sides have the same length.

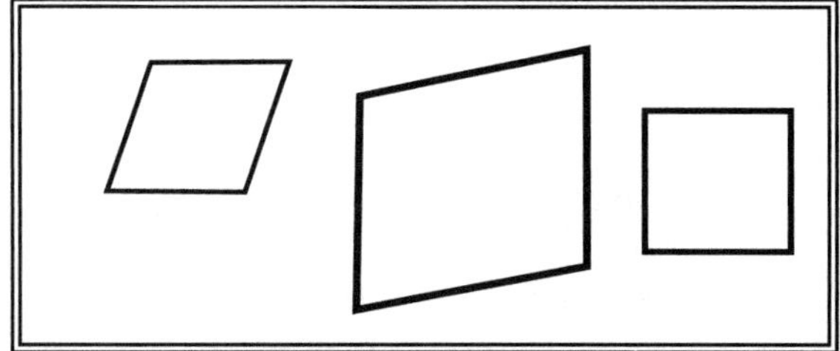

Each of these is a rhombus.

end of small essay

Your Turn to Play

1. Find the silent letter in each of these words:
   - listen
   - choir
   - knee
   - wrist

2. Find three errors in this letter.

Deer Jennifer,

I really want to go to Australia to help people.

Yours Truly.

Fred

.......ANSWERS.......

1. lis_t_en
   c_h_oir
   _k_nee
   _w_rist

2. (error #1) The words *deer* and *dear* sound alike, but they have different meanings.

deer = 

(error #2) Only the first word in a closing salutation is capitalized. A lot of adults make this mistake.

(error #3) The closing salutation always ends with a comma.

Dear Jennifer,

I really want to go to Australia to help people.

Yours truly,

Fred

Chapter Seven
Packing

Fred began to pack for his trip. His clothes were the easiest thing to pack. He started at his feet and worked his way up to his head. He needed his jogging shoes and a pair of nice shoes that he would use for teaching. Socks. Pants and underpants. Shirts. Bow ties. Fred liked to wear a bow tie when he was teaching.

❀ ❀ ❀

Wait a minute! I, your reader, have a question. You, Mr. Author, did not answer the question.

What question?

Fred said that Australia was a giant island. Kingie didn't want to argue with Fred about whether it is an island or a continent. I need to know. Which is it?

Couldn't we just forget about the island-continent debate and get back to Fred packing for his trip?

No! I bought this book, and I demand an answer.

But I don't know the answer. I can't even tell you what an island is.

Yes you can. Anybody knows what an island is. It is a hunk of land completely surrounded by water. That's easy.

It's not that easy. Take a globe of the world and look at the South Pole. The South Pole is on the continent of Antarctica.

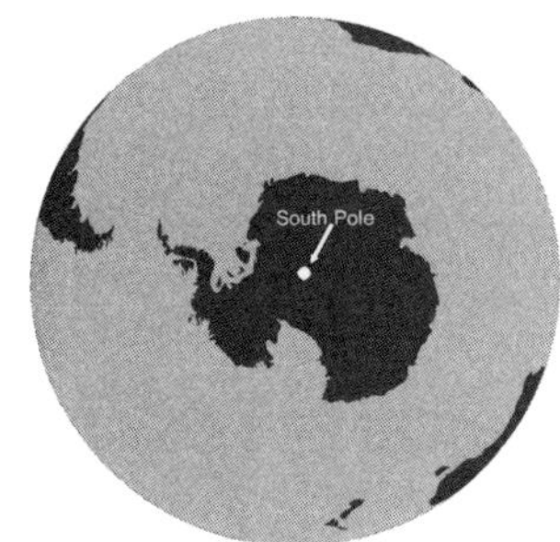

Antarctica (ant-ARK-tick-ka) is completely surrounded by water, but no geographer calls Antarctica an island.

Okay. Do you have ANY idea what a continent is?

Sure. The seven continents are North America, South America, Asia, Europe, Africa, Australia, and Antarctica. That's what they taught me in school.

Hey! Stop it! I'm asking why they call those things continents. There is a difference between what things are continents and why they are called continents.*

---

* Do you remember the six question words: *what, why, when, where, who,* and *how?*

Okay. While Fred is picking out which bow ties he wants to take, I'll tell you what Kingie was afraid to mention.

You have to answer four questions if you want to know if something is a continent.

Question #1: Are the plants and animals different from other places on earth?

Question #2: Does it sit on its own tectonic plate? South America sits on one tectonic plate. Africa sits on another. Very slowly, these plates are moving.

Question #3: Is the culture different from other continents?

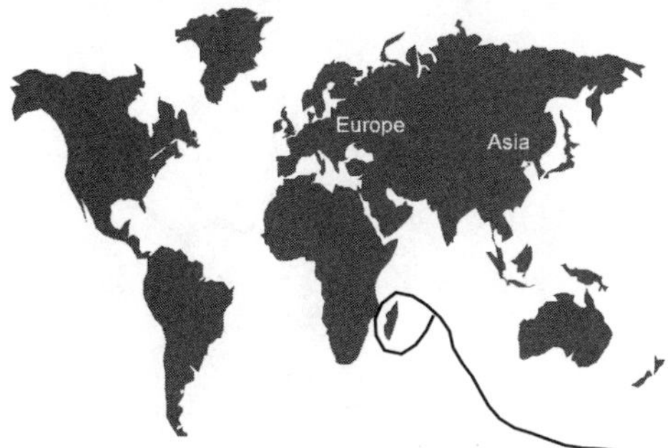

The cultures of Europe and Asia are much more different from each other than the cultures of Germany and France (both of which are in Europe).

Question #4: Do the local people say they are on a separate continent?

So I, your reader, need to know the final answer.

Australia has unique plants and animals. Yes to question one.

Australia is on its own tectonic plate. Yes to question two. Madagascar is also on its own tectonic plate, but nobody calls it a continent.

Australia has ancient cultures found nowhere else. Yes to question three.

Telephone Australians and ask them, "Is Australia the world's largest island or is it the world's smallest continent?" They can't agree with each other. Some say one thing and some say the other. Yes and no to question four.

Now do you see why Kingie was smart not to get into a discussion with Fred about whether Australia is a continent?

I do. Thank you for answering my question.

❀ ❀ ❀

Fred picked out lots of math bow ties that he thought that would be perfect when he taught in Australia.

It had taken Fred about five minutes to pack all the clothes that he needed. Five-year-old boys don't think about clothes as much as 15-year-old girls do.

What was important to Fred was teaching. He wanted to help some of the people of Australia by teaching them all the math that he knew. He packed pencils, paper, clipboards, rulers, and lots of math books.

He packed arithmetic books, algebra books, geometry books, trig books, and calculus books. He packed books about set theory, about logic, and about topology.* Fred wanted to be ready to teach any kind of math that his students needed.

easy arithmetic book

Your Turn to Play

1. *Deer* and *dear* sound alike but mean different things. *Deer* and *dear* are called **homonyms**.**
   What is a homonym for *their*?
2. What is a homonym for *hear*?
3. Find the silent letter in each of these words:
   half raspberry whole

---

* Topology (tah-PALL-ah-jee) is an advanced math course studied in college. High school geometry studies circles and squares (○ and □). Topology is "stretchy" geometry. In topology, since you can stretch a circle into a square, they say that a circle and a square are the same thing. Topology is weird.

** Some people also call them homophones. English can be very messy, just like geography.

.......ANSWERS.......

1. There are two homonyms for *their*: *there* and *they're*.

2. *Here* is a homonym for *hear*.
3. ha*l*f
   ras*p*berry
   *w*hole

And, of course, *whole* and *hole* are homonyms.

Can you toss a whole house in a hole?

Chapter Eight
How to Get There

Fred knew he couldn't take a bus from Kansas to Australia. The Pacific Ocean separated North America from Australia.

He couldn't take a train.

There were two reasons why he couldn't take an ocean cruise to get there. The first reason was that Kansas is in the middle of the United States. No ocean liner can travel over land.

⇦ silly picture

The second reason Fred couldn't use a ship to get to Australia was that he had only two days to get there.

He would have to fly.

Today was Sunday. He needed to be there by Tuesday. He knew that he shouldn't wait until Monday to get his plane ticket. As the old saying goes, "*Never leave till tomorrow what you can do today.*"

If he waited until Monday, he would never have gotten to Australia on time. The first leg of the trip was the afternoon bus to Wichita,

(WHICH-eh-taw) Kansas. Then he would fly from there to Los Angeles. After a two-hour layover, he would change to another plane and fly to Australia.*

Fred walked over to watch Kingie work on a new oil painting. Kingie had started by drawing in pencil.

pencil sketch

"Who's** that?" Fred asked.

"That's my sketch of Daniel Boone," Kingie said. "Everybody who knows any American history has heard of him. He was an explorer and trail maker. In 1775 he blazed a trail, which he called his Wilderness Road, into Kentucky.

---

* In the 1950s, Fred would have probably gone to a travel agent to make the arrangements. In 2010, he would have used his computer or, more recently, his super all-in-one smart phone with 4,038,923 applications.

By the time your grandchildren read this book, Fred might just spit on the ground and talk to his spit to make the reservations. The future is very hard to predict nowadays.

** *Who's* and *whose* are homonyms. *Who's* is an abbreviation for "who is."

Question: Whose painting is that? Answer: Kingie owns that painting.
Question: Who's in the painting? Answer: Daniel Boone.

That's one year before Congress adopted the Declaration of Independence (July 4, 1776)."

Fred didn't understand. "What does blazing a trail mean?" Fred knew a lot about math, but he had never studied much history.

Kingie explained, "Boone had to cut his way through thick bushes and dense forests to make a trail that others could follow to get to Kentucky."

"I guess I'm a trailblazer to Australia."

Kingie shouted, "NO. YOU ARE NOT DANIEL BOONE! Lots of people travel to Australia. You are not the first."

Time Out!

But Fred was a trailblazer. No other five-year-old had ever been called by the Mission Board to go and teach anywhere.

The Mission Board didn't know that Fred was so young. They thought that because he had been teaching at the university for five years, he was at least in his late 20s.

Kingie was only a six-inch tall doll, but he knew about some things that Fred didn't.

The first leg of Fred's trip was a bus trip to Wichita. Fred gave Kingie a hug and walked out of his office,

down the hallway,

down two flights of stairs,

across the KITTENS campus,

and to the bus station.

The sign in the bus station read:

SUNDAY BUS TO WICHITA LEAVES AT 3 P.M.

Fred was happy that it was 3 p.m. and not 3 a.m.* Fred looked at the clock on the wall. He had one hour to wait.

two o'clock

Perfect! Fred thought. *I have some time to read.* He pulled out the geometry book that he had packed. *The Mission Board might want me to teach geometry when I get to Australia.*

---

* p.m. means in the afternoon or evening—any time between noon and midnight.

a.m. means morning—any time between midnight and noon. Noon and midnight are neither a.m. nor p.m.

Fred loved to read. His favorite things to do were:

to teach,

to read,

to spend time with his friends Betty and Alexander,

to jog in the early morning, and

to sing.

Your Turn to Play

1. Let's play You Are the Teacher.

Find three errors in this letter.

Dear Kingie,

I am hear at the bus station right now. I miss you. the bus will come in one hour.

Love:

Fred

2. Draw a picture of something you like to do.

.......ANSWERS.......

1. (error #1) The words *hear* and *here* sound alike, but they have different meanings.

(error #2) It should be *The bus* and not *the bus*. Every sentence begins with a capital letter.

(error #3) The closing salutation always ends with a comma.

Dear Kingie,

I am here at the bus station right now. I miss you. The bus will come in one hour.

Love,

Fred

2. Everyone's picture will be different. I, your author, like the things that Fred likes, but I also like eating pizza, hugging my wife, and taking naps.

Chapter Nine
On the Bus

Fred's geometry book had drawings of many four-sided figures. He couldn't decide which one was his favorite.

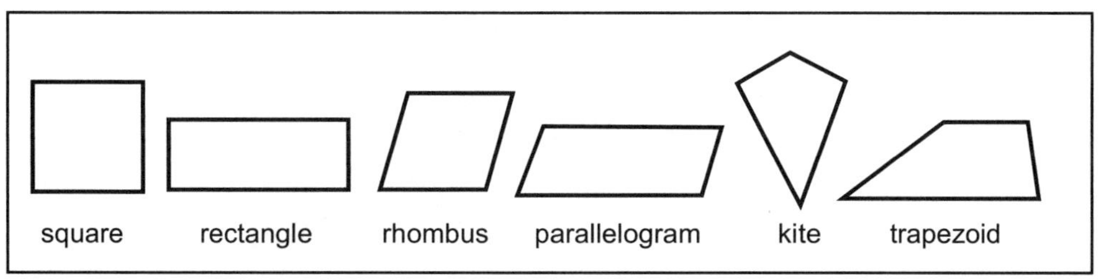

They left one out! Fred thought to himself. *Books are not perfect. They are just like people. They can make mistakes.*

I can think of a four-sided figure that is:

- ✻ *not a square* (four equal sides and four equal angles)
- ✻ *not a rectangle* (four equal angles)
- ✻ *not a rhombus* (four equal sides)
- ✻ *not a parallelogram* (opposite sides parallel)
- ✻ *not a kite and* (two pairs of adjacent equal sides) (adjacent = next to)
- ✻ *not a trapezoid.* (exactly one pair of parallel sides)

Fred drew

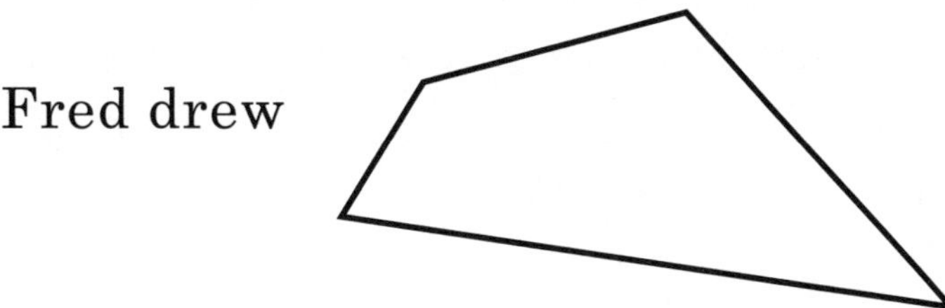

The bus came. It was three o'clock. Fred's mind was on geometry. He noticed the parallel lines that were painted on the side of the bus.

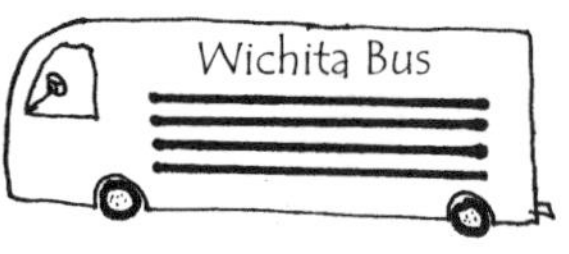

Fred suddenly realized that there was no way to get on the bus. There was no door.

Fred panicked.

Fred's thoughts switched from geometry to, *Oh, no. If I can't get on the bus, how will I ever get to Australia?*

A little tear ran down Fred's cheek.

"Hey, kid!" the bus driver said. "Everyone else is on board. We've got to get going."

Fred followed the bus driver around to the other side of the bus. Fred discovered a secret about buses:

Secret ⇨ Buses have doors only on one side.

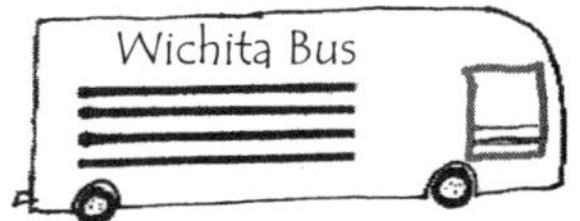

The driver helped Fred load all his stuff onto the bus, and they were off to Wichita.

Fred headed to the back of the bus so that he could look out the back window. He thought, *I can see where we have been, and the driver can see where we are going.*

As the bus headed down the highway, Fred had fun waving to the cows that they passed. None of them waved back, but Fred thought that he saw one of them smile.

Then he started to have trouble seeing out the back window. Everything was getting darker and darker. This seemed strange because it was only a little after three o'clock.

Fred walked to the front of the bus and looked out the front window. Everything was bright and clear.

Before Fred could ask the driver why it was nighttime in the back of the bus and daytime in the front of the bus, another passenger yelled, "Hey, driver! You have a smoking bus. You're probably killing the cows in the field."

Here is what Fred imagined.

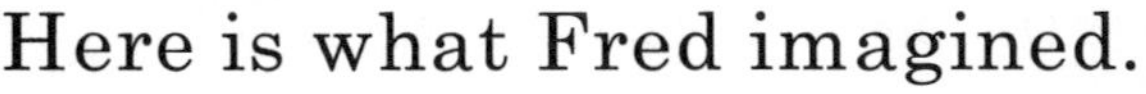

But no cows were being killed. The passenger was just exaggerating. He didn't mean that cows were literally being hurt.

small essay

Telling the Truth

The passenger was not lying when he talked about dead cows. The important thing is that the driver knew he was just exaggerating. Lying only happens when you are trying to deceive someone.

When your mother says, "I have told you a million times to clean up your room," she is not lying. Both she and you know that if she told you to clean up your room every day from the day you were born until you turned 18, she would have only told you 6,570 times.* That is a lot less than 1,000,000.

Exaggerated speech is called **hyperbole** (high-PERB-a-lee). Almost everyone uses hyperbole: mothers, authors, kids.

Have you ever heard someone say, "I bet you a million dollars that . . ."? That's hyperbole.

The car salesman says, "This is the perfect car for you." That's hyperbole. You know that he is exaggerating. It may be an excellent car, but only God is perfect.

The difficulty with using hyperbole occurs when the listener doesn't realize that you are exaggerating. When Fred heard about dying cows, he didn't realize the passenger was speaking hyperbolically.

end of small essay

---

* On the day you turned 18, you would have lived 18 years. 18 years × 365 days/year = 6,570 days. (It would be a little more if you count leap years.)

Your Turn to Play

1. (multiple-choice question)

How many cows were really being killed by the bus's smoke?

A) zero cows

B) one cow

C) many cows

2. (true-false question)

The cows are very happy smelling the bus smoke.

Smiling cows?

3. Draw a picture of an unhappy cow.

.......ANSWERS.......

1. The correct answer is A) zero cows.

2. False. Smelling smoke does not make cows happy.

Smelling smoke does not make a firefighter happy. It means that there is a fire that needs to be put out.

Smelling smoke does not make a cook happy. That means some food is burning.

Smelling smoke is the worst smell in the world. (hyperbole)

3. Here is Fred's attempt to draw an unhappy cow.

Chapter Ten
Replacing the Bus *that* Smoked

The bus driver pulled the bus over to the side of the road and stopped. He scratched his head and asked, "Does anybody have a cell phone that I can borrow?"*

Nine people offered him their phones.

Twenty-three people on the bus had cell phones, but there were only nine who were willing to lend their phones to the driver. The phrase "that I can borrow" was an important part of the sentence.

The driver called his boss, "Hey, George. We have trouble here. This is the Wichita bus

---

* *That* and *which* are often confused with each other.

☞ Use *that* when it is vital, when it is needed to define the thing it is referring to.

☞ Use *which* when it is just adding additional information, when it is just an add-on.

I want to vote for someone that is honest.

(Without the "that is honest," the sentence becomes, "I want to vote for someone." "That is honest" is vital to the meaning of the sentence.)

I like anchovy pizza, which can be purchased at several stores in my town.

(Without the "which can be purchased at several stores in my town," the sentence still makes sense: "I like anchovy pizza." The *which* clause is just an add-on.)

and it's really smoking. This is bus #59. Do you have any ideas?"

George said, "I know what happened. You grabbed the wrong bus this morning. Number 59, which we call Old Smoker, was supposed to be in the repair shop today. You should have taken #72. I'll bring #72 to you." (Notice that "which we call Old Smoker" is an add-on. Leaving it out doesn't change the meaning of the sentence.)

Fred looked at the clock on the wall of the bus. It was ten minutes after three.

3:10

At twenty minutes after three, George arrived.

3:20

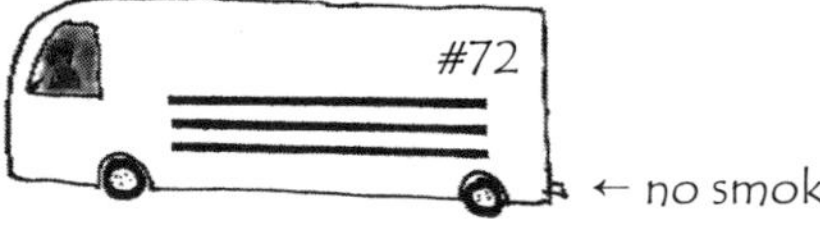

Everyone got off Old Smoker and onto #72. Everyone remembered to take their baggage from the old bus to the new one.

Everyone, except . . . Fred.

Fred was now heading to Australia with no extra clothes and no math books.

He headed to the back of the bus and lay down for a little nap. As the old saying goes, "*He headed off to the Land of Nod.*"

Meanwhile, George drove Old Smoker to the repair shop. When he got there, he noticed

Fred's suitcase and his boxes of books. Fortunately, Fred had labeled the boxes and put a tag on his suitcase that listed his name and address.

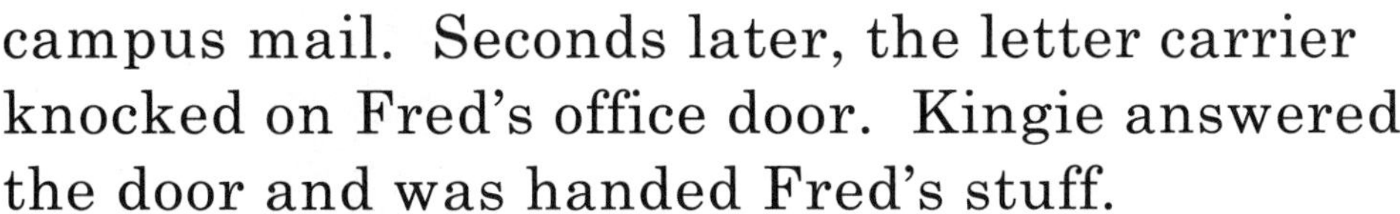

George put the suitcase and the boxes into the KITTENS campus mail. Seconds later, the letter carrier knocked on Fred's office door. Kingie answered the door and was handed Fred's stuff.

Kingie is a beanbag doll that Fred got from King of French Fries years ago.

Kingie had no idea why all of Fred's things were mailed back to his office. It was a mystery.

Kingie went back to oil painting. There was no use worrying since there was nothing that he could do about the situation.

Fred wasn't worried either. He was asleep and dreaming about owning a pet store. He dreamed that the store had dogs, cats, monkeys, and fish. *(When you have a list of three or more things, you put commas between the items.)*

He dreamed that he took the dogs, cats, and monkeys out of their cages and let them run around in the store. He didn't take the fish out of their tanks.

The dogs and cats *(two items and no comma)* played. The monkeys hit the keys on the cash register.

There were also some parakeets, canaries, and parrots. Fred opened their cage doors. The parakeets and canaries *(no comma)* flew out. The parrots just sat there.

It was a dream, so it didn't matter to Fred that the parakeet was as large as the cat or that the cat was wearing pants.

Your Turn to Play

1. Put commas in this sentence:

The cat ate the fish the canary and the parakeet.

2. Put commas in this sentence:

Fred dreamed he could fly in the sky swim under water and quack like a duck.

3. Insert *that* or *which* into each blank.

Fred dreamed about an animal _____ hit keys on a cash register.

The monkey, _____ was born in Iowa, liked to play the piano.

Any monkey _____ plays the piano is a special monkey.

.......ANSWERS.......

1. The cat ate the fish, the canary, and the parakeet.

2. Fred dreamed he could fly in the sky, swim under water, and quack like a duck.

3.

Fred dreamed about an animal <u>that</u> hit keys on a cash register.

"Hit keys on a cash register" defines which animal we are talking about.

The monkey, <u>which</u> was born in Iowa, liked to play the piano.

If you leave out "which was born in Iowa," the sentence still makes sense. "Which was born in Iowa" is an add-on.

Any monkey <u>that</u> plays the piano is a special monkey.

If you leave out "that plays the piano," you change the meaning of the sentence. "That plays the piano" defines the monkey we are talking about.

Chapter Eleven
Wichita

The bus driver announced, "Wichita." In Fred's dream all the animals rushed back into their cages, and then Fred woke up. He liked to have very neat dreams. As the old saying goes, "*A place for everything and everything in its place.*"

Fred's office was like that. All the books were arranged on his bookshelves by subject.

The math books were in one section. The poetry books were in another section.

His pens and pencils were kept in one desk drawer. The top of his desk was clear when he wasn't working on something.

No baby ever cleans up after himself. Few five-year-olds ever keep things neat. Some teenagers and some adults only straighten things out when important company is coming.

Some of the other teachers at KITTENS University had very messy offices. Their desktops were filled with papers, half-empty cups of coffee, and unopened letters that were three weeks old.

This is not how Fred kept his office.

As everyone got off the bus, Fred realized that he had left his stuff on Old Smoker. This didn't bother Fred very much for three reasons.

✱ First, he still had his airplane tickets and his money ($12) in his wallet.

✱ Second, because he had been teaching math for many years at KITTENS University, he knew the math and really didn't need all the books he had brought.

✱ Third, five-year-olds and fifteen-year-olds are very different when it comes to clothing.

Five-year-olds	Fifteen-year-olds
They wear clothes because everyone else wears clothes.	Modesty becomes important.
Their clothes can get dirty, muddy, ripped. Kids' sweat glands produce only water and salt.	As kids turn into adults they get a second set of sweat glands, which produce water, salt, and proteins. After a day or so, the proteins can start to smell bad. Fifteen-year-olds either need to ① bathe, ② use deodorants, or ③ change their stinky clothes.

Time Out!

Did you notice Kids' sweat glands?

It's not Kids's.

English is filled with weird rules. This is a rule that many adults don't know.

We write . . .

Pat's lunch
Iris's dog
men's room
children's toys
Venus's beauty
dress's hem

But . . .

kids' sweat
tourists' bags
states' rights
mothers' dreams
} no s after the apostrophe!
(uh-POS-tro-fee)

The Rule: You need two things in order to omit the s after the apostrophe:

❶ The word must be plural (more than one).

Here are some plural words: kids, toys, women, pizzas, songs, books, marbles, pencils.

❷ The word must end in s.

Here are some words that end in s: trucks, mess, dress, leaves, Louis, companies

If the word is both plural and ends in s, skip the s after the apostrophe.

❀ ❀ ❀

Fred was at the bus station, and he needed to get to the Wichita airport. He asked the taxi driver, "How do I get to the airport?"

The driver, whose name was C.C. Coalback, said, "Get in. I'll drive you there."

Fred got in. As the old saying goes, "*Fred was a fish out of water.**" Fred should have asked some important questions before he got in the taxi.

---

* *Fish out of water* = to be in a strange or uncomfortable place

Coalback drove him to the airport and said, "That will be $5."

Fred paid him and got out of the taxi.

The airport was one block from the bus stop. The taxi ride had taken one minute.

Your Turn to Play

1. Find the silent letter in each of these words:

   cocoa

   scene

   sign

2. Which is right? This question is not easy. Many high school students would not know the correct answers.

   women's shoes
   women' shoes

   doctor's wife
   doctors' wife

   nurses' wives (Nurses can be men.)
   nurses's wives

.......ANSWERS.......

1. cocoa

scene

sign

2. women's shoes
women' shoes

women's shoes because the word did not end in s.

doctor's wife
doctors' wife

doctor's wife because doctor was not plural.

nurses' wives
nurses's wives

nurses' wives because nurses was both plural and ended in s. We knew that nurses was plural, because one nurse couldn't have *wives*.

A note from the author: Please do not feel bad if you had trouble with question 2. You are doing fine if you can tell me what is wrong with:

Jason'ssss bike too many s's

Margaret'''s computer too many apostrophes

Chapter Twelve
Ask

Fred now had seven dollars left. He should have asked the taxi driver questions such as, "How far is it to the airport?" or "How much will the ride cost?"

12
– 5
7

If you are thinking about getting a job, you should ask questions such as, "What will I be doing?" or "How much is the salary?" You might find out that you might have to wrestle rattlesnakes and get paid $1 a week.

If you are thinking about marrying someone, you might ask questions such as, "Do you like children?" You might find out that that person really hates kids.

If you are thinking about anything,
ask questions!

Fred had arrived at the Wichita Mid-Continent Airport, the largest and busiest airport in Kansas. He knew he needed to get to Los Angeles, but he wasn't sure where the airline was located. He walked past the information booth and wandered down the East Concourse, which

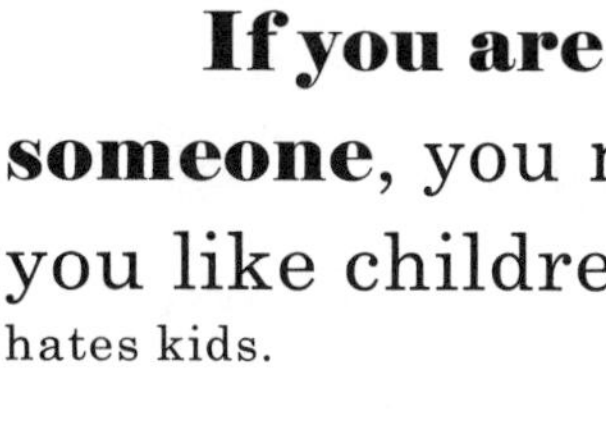

INFO

Fred didn't ask

houses Gates 1 through 6. He didn't find the airline he needed. He walked down the West Concourse. After 20 minutes of walking he found the airline that he was looking for. It was near the information booth.

He handed his ticket to the airline host. He told Fred, "It will be several moments before you can board the plane. Passengers need to deplane first."

Fred didn't know what *deplane* meant. He imagined that it meant to get rid of the plane. He was confusing *deplane* with *demolish*. He pictured all of the passengers going out to the plane and hitting it with hammers.

He looked out the window and saw passengers getting off the plane.* No one was hitting the plane with hammers.

Soon it was time for Fred and the other departing passengers to board the plane. Everyone else had purses, backpacks, or small suitcases. (Notice the commas.)

Fred had nothing to carry.

---

* That's what *deplane* means. *Boarding a plane* means getting on a plane.

When he boarded the plane, the flight attendant looked at him and asked, "Are you flying alone?" She was concerned about this small child flying without any adult to take care of him.

Fred thought that was a silly question. He said, "No. All these other people are also going to Los Angeles."

Fred headed down the aisle (two silent letters: a and s) and climbed into a seat. He liked the fact that there was plenty of room in those chairs. He could lie down and take a nap if he wanted to.

The 300-pound man next to him could barely squeeze into his chair.

The flight attendant announced, "Everybody please put on your seat belts. We are about to take off."

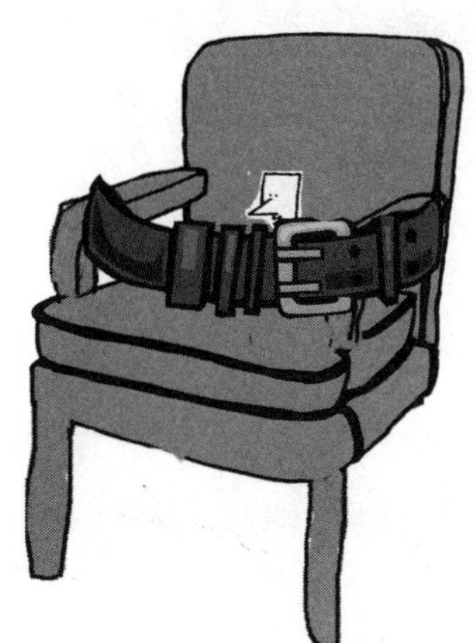

Fred felt very secure.

But he couldn't move his arms.

After takeoff, the flight attendant came by and loosened Fred's seat belt. That was much better.

There was a choice of shows that he could watch:

✧ Romance (Five-year-old Fred wasn't interested.)
✧ Wrestling (a silent *t*)
✧ War (He didn't like to see people hurt.)
✧ Science (Yes!)

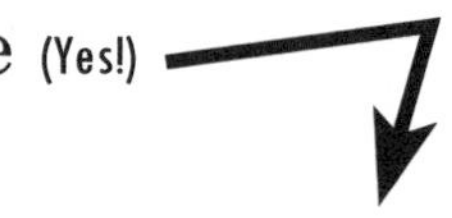

Welcome to the Science Show!
Today's topic is the compass.

Fred thought they were going to talk about the kind of compass that is used to draw circles. When Fred taught geometry at KITTENS, every student had a compass.

We are going to talk about compasses used by hikers to tell which direction is north. If you are hiking and you want to head toward the top of the map, you want to head north.

Your compass will point to the north.

Fred thought *It would be fun to have a compass.*

Compasses have a little magnet inside that points toward the magnetic north pole, which is different than the true north pole.

Then things in the program got really complicated.

The magnetic north pole was discovered in 1831. It's moving! Up to 1970 it was moving at about 9 km* per year. After 1970 it started moving at about 41 km per year. In 2009 it was moving at about 58 km per year—the fastest in human history.

Airport runways are named by their compass directions. Runways across the United States have had to rename all their runways at least once every five years!

And a little scary . . .

Some experts are suggesting that the Earth's magnetic field is getting ready to "flip"—north may become south, and south may become north. It's called a pole reversal. ". . . at least several hundred [pole reversals] have happened."**

Your Turn to Play

1. Insert *that* or *which* in each blank.

Airport runways ____ have the wrong compass directions would be dangerous.

Renaming airport runways, ____ is an expensive process, must be done.

2. Which is correct? the compass's pointy end / the compass' pointy end

---

* 1 km = 1 kilometer, which is a little over a half mile.

** E.D. Hirsch, Jr., *The Dictionary of Cultural Literacy*, 2nd edition, p. 501

. . . . ANSWERS . . . .

1. Airport runways <u>that</u> have the wrong compass directions would be dangerous.

If you leave out "that have the wrong compass directions," the sentence doesn't make any sense. The phrase "that have the wrong compass directions" defines the particular runways we are talking about.

Renaming airport runways, <u>which</u> is an expensive process, must be done.

"Which is an expensive process" is an add-on. If you take it out, the sentence still makes sense.

Pilots' maps show the layouts of each airport that they are going to land at. Most airports have more than one runway. Part of the description of each runway is the compass direction (something like 82.7°N 114.4°W).

In pilot school they teach that it is really nice to land on the correct runway, otherwise, you might crash into another plane, which isn't very desirable.

You may have noticed by now that phrases beginning with *which* are separated from the rest of the sentence by commas. This shows that they are add-ons that are not essential to the meaning of the sentence.

Renaming airport runways, <u>which</u> is an expensive process, must be done.

2. the compass's pointy end

In order to drop the *s* you need a plural word that ends in *s*.

We are talking about one compass. It is not plural.

One compass. Two compasses. compasses' pointy ends

Chapter Thirteen
Flying

Fred turned off the show. He was afraid to hear any more. He was afraid that during his flight to the Los Angeles International Airport a pole reversal would happen and the pilot would get lost. Fred hid under his seat belt.

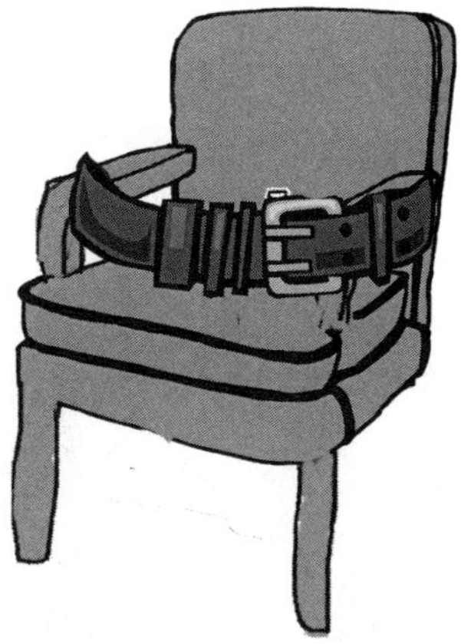

If Fred had listened to the program for just one more minute, he would have heard Jeffrey Love of the U.S. Geological Survey say, "Reversals typically take about 10,000 years to happen."*

Fred did not have to worry.

Halfway through the flight, the attendants came down the aisle offering cans of Sluice to any of the passengers who wanted one. Sluice is the world's sweetest soft drink. It has so much sugar in it that it is thick like syrup.

---

* Jeffrey Love is a real person. He actually said this. The U.S. Geological Survey is real. And pole reversals are also real.

The attendant couldn't see Fred. She thought that he might have gone to the restroom. She left a can of Sluice for him. She thought that Fred's head was a table top.

Because Fred's head was so flat and he was so short, people would continually* mistake him for a small table.

The 300-pound man next to Fred thought the can was for him. He drank it and put the empty can back on Fred's head.

The flight attendant came by and removed the empty can.

---

* Some people mix up **continual** with **continuous**. Both mean that something is happening all the time.

Continual means that it's always occurring with obvious breaks. ----------- ------ ---------- ----------- -------- -------------- ---- ----------- ------- ---- -------

Continuous means without any breaks. ------------ ---

The baby was continually crying during the first year of his life. (He didn't cry when sleeping or eating.)

The baby cried continuously for ten minutes. (He didn't take a single break.)

Fred felt the top of his head. It was sticky. He knew that he would have to wash it when he got to Los Angeles.

An announcement came: "This is your pilot. We are now approaching the Los Angeles International Airport. Please fasten (silent *t*) your seat belt. I hope you have had a wonderful flight with us."

Fred hadn't.

The man put his paper napkin on Fred's head. He hadn't realized that there was a little boy sitting next to him.

Fred tried to remove the napkin. It shredded in his hands. Sluice made an excellent glue.

There were little bits of paper all over Fred's lap and his chair.

After Fred deplaned, the cleanup crew knew exactly where the five-year-old boy had been sitting.

Fred's first stop after he got off the airplane was the restroom. He wanted to be **less** conspicuous. He wanted **fewer** people to be looking at him and giggling.*

---

* *Less* and *fewer*. Use *fewer* when you can count them.
less sugar and fewer spoons

He walked down the concourse. When he came close to the restroom, he saw the sign:

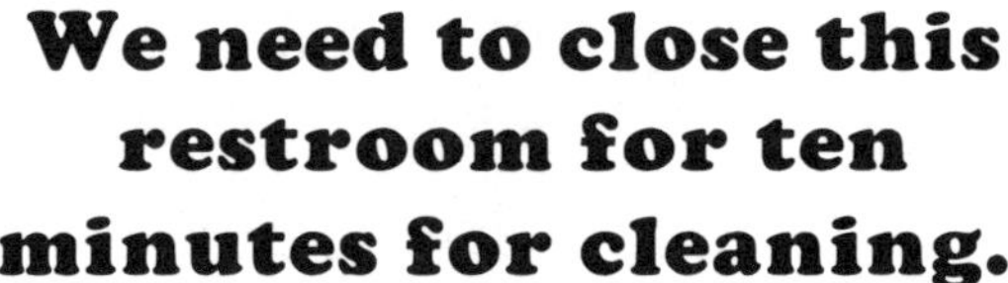

While Fred stood there waiting, we need to have a . . .

Time Out!

Did you just notice something?

. . . he came *close* to the restroom
. . . need to *close* this restroom

The first *close* sounds a little like *toast*.
The second *close* sounds like *clothes*.

They are spelled the same.
They sound different.
They have different meanings.
These two words are heteronyms.
(HET-er-eh-nims)

He tried to *lead* them, but their feet were made of *lead*.
He did not *object* when he was made the *object* of ridicule.
The *wind* was strong. It made it hard to *wind* up the rope.
Don't *tear* my drawing or I will shed a *tear*.

Your Turn to Play

1. Which one of these three sentences contains a pair of heteronyms?

   A) The treaty, a *piece* of paper, meant there would be *peace*.

   B) It was time to *present* his *present*.

   C) It was *too* hard *to* run *two* miles.

2. Which is correct?
   - the ladies' restroom
   - the ladies's restroom

3. Insert *that* or *which* in the blank.

   Heteronyms are two words _____ are spelled the same but sound different and have different meanings.

. . . . ANSWERS . . . .

1. B) It was time to *present* his *present.*

These two words are spelled the same but sound different and have different meanings.

The first *present* means to give something.
The second *present* means a gift.

Spelled the same = heteronyms

Sounds the same = homonyms piece and peace; too, to, and two

(Homonyms were mentioned in Chapter 8.)

2. the ladies' restroom

The word *ladies* is plural and ends in s. Those are the two things needed in order to omit the s after the apostrophe.

3. Heteronyms are two words _that_ are spelled the same but sound different and have different meanings.

We use *that* when the words that follow the *that* are essential to the meaning of the sentence.

Suppose we left out the *that* phrase. The sentence would read: Heteronyms are two words. That would be pretty silly.

Chapter Fourteen
Lost

After the cleaning crew removed the sign, Fred ran into the restroom, turned on the faucet, and put his head under the water. He washed off the shredded paper napkin. That felt good. The Sluice and paper napkin had been starting to itch.

He dried his head with a paper towel. The paper towel did not stick to his head because he had washed off the sticky Sluice.

As he left the restroom, he saw a map of the Los Angeles International Airport on the wall.

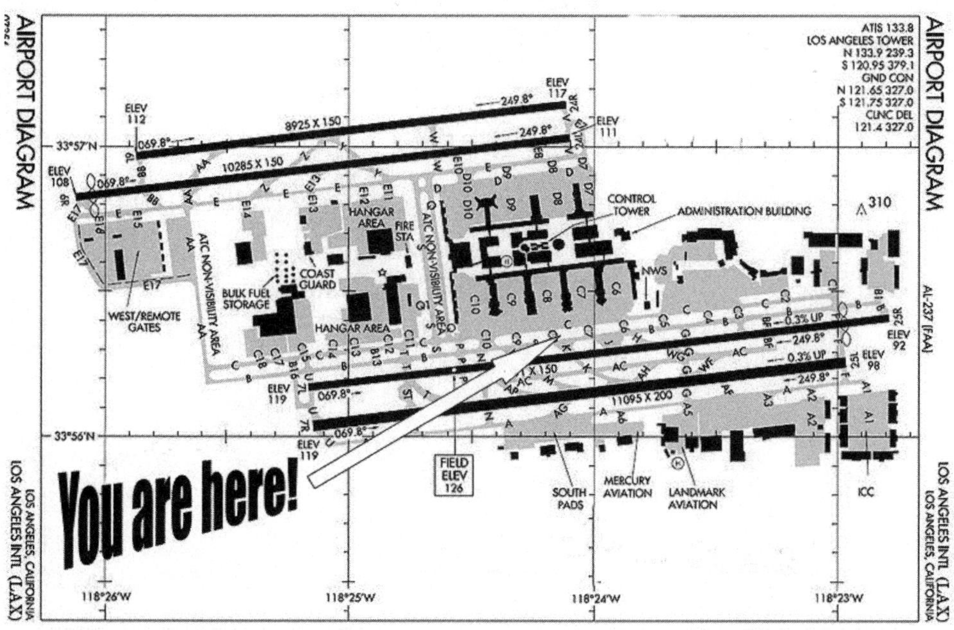

It wasn't exactly clear how to get to the airline that would take Fred to Australia. (This is called an understatement.) The plain truth was that Fred had no idea where to head. All he knew was that he had two hours to switch from his plane from Kansas to the plane that would take him to Australia. Plain and plane are homonyms.

The Los Angeles International Airport is the sixth busiest airport in the world. It is big.

Fred had two choices. He could go and ask someone for directions, or he could sit down on the floor and cry.

When you are

- five years old
- three feet tall
- weigh 37 pounds
- have no luggage and only $7
- are alone in a huge airport and
- are totally lost

the only logical thing to do would be to sit on the floor and cry.

Fred was logical.*

---

* Next year, when Fred turns six, he will go and ask for help.

"Are you lost, little fellow?" a woman asked. "I have three grandchildren that are your age."

Fred pointed to the map. He knew that he wasn't lost. The map told him where he was. He just didn't know where anything else was.

"Where are your parents?" she asked.

Fred said, "It's been over four years since I've seen them." He was telling the truth, but the grandmother thought he was exaggerating.

An airport security officer walked by. The grandmother called to him, "Could you help us?"

Fred liked the way she asked the question. She could have said, "Could you help this poor little lost boy?"

Fred showed him his airline ticket. The officer took his hand and the pair walked to the correct airline gate. The sign read:

BOARDING IN 20 MINUTES FOR SYDNEY, AUSTRALIA

Fred felt relieved. He was in the right spot. He knew that there was no direct flight from Los Angeles to the Wagga Wagga Airport. His whole trip would be: KITTENS University ➟ Wichita, Kansas ➟ Los Angeles, California ➟ Sydney, Australia ➟ Wagga Wagga, Australia.

Fred thanked the officer.

It was late Sunday night. He needed to get to Wagga Wagga by Tuesday. He was right on schedule.

There was a big map of Australia on the wall. From a distance, Fred couldn't see Wagga Wagga.

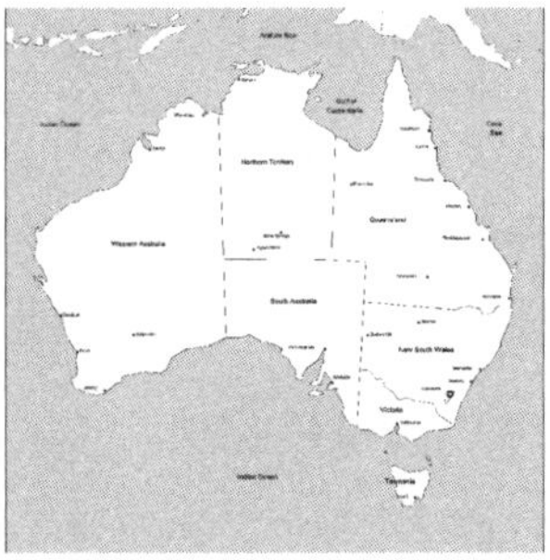

He walked up closer to the map. He knew that Wagga Wagga was in the southeastern part of Australia.

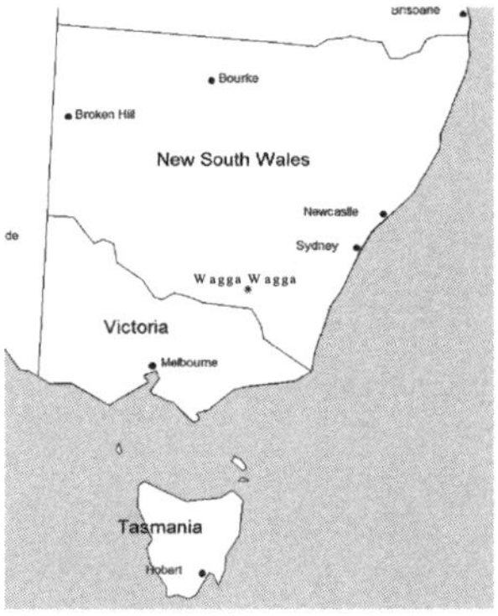

There it was. It was halfway between Melbourne and Sydney.

Wagga Wagga is a large inland city in Australia. Fred was eager to begin teaching there. He remembered what the board chairman, Jennifer Glory, had written, "We have a great need for an experienced teacher such as you for the summer."

The quotation marks that come at the end of a quotation are called **close-quotes**.

Periods and commas go to the left of close-quotes.*

"I was thinking," Sam said, "of buying a new car."

Your Turn to Play

1. Write a homonym (sounds alike) for each of these words:

marry Will you marry me?

bear I saw a bear at the zoo.

rode I rode the horse.

2. Add commas and/or periods:

"I'm thirsty" she said

She said, "Green is good" and the monkey did a little dance

---

* In some other countries they do things differently. They even spell words differently. In some places they write *colour* instead of *color* and *grey* instead of *gray.*

.......ANSWERS.......

1. merry merry Christmas or Mary had a little lamb.
   bare the cupboard was bare*
   road cars on the road or rowed the boat

2. "I'm thirsty," she said.
   She said, "Green is good," and the monkey did a little dance.

---

*A nursery rhyme:

Old Mother Hubbard
Went to the cupboard,
  To get her poor dog a bone,
But when she got there,
The cupboard was bare,
  And so her poor dog had none.

Chapter Fifteen
Boarding

Fred heard the announcement: "We are now boarding for our flight to Australia. Families with small children may board first."

Fred listened carefully. He didn't want to get in trouble. The announcement said, "families with small children," and he wasn't a family with small children. He waited.

"Those individuals in wheelchairs or who have difficulty walking may board now." Fred knew that this did not apply to him. He waited.

"Adults may now board." Fred waited.

He was the only one who had not gotten on the plane. He wondered if there would be an announcement, "Five-year-olds who teach mathematics at KITTENS University may board now." No such announcement was made.

Instead, "Last call. We will be shutting the doors in one minute." Fred ran and boarded the plane just before the flight attendant closed the door.

His ticket said Seat 5B, but the 300-pound man was sitting in 5B. Fred should have asked, but instead, he just sat on the floor.

The flight attendant knelt* down and asked Fred if he needed help. He handed her his ticket and pointed to the man in 5B. He was afraid to speak.

The attendant smiled, picked Fred up, and put him in seat 5B. The big man was sitting in seat 5D.

She fastened his seat belt and said, "Have a nice day."

---

* To *kneel* means to go down on one or both knees. Both *kneel* and *knees* have silent k's.

Present tense Right now I kneel.
Past tense Yesterday I knelt.

Present tense Today I sing.
Past tense Last week I sang.

Present tense I eat a pizza.
Past tense Last month I ate seven pizzas.

The weird thing in English is that *kneel* has two ways of indicating its past tense. You can say either She knelt or She kneeled. Both are correct. English is harder than math.

Have a nice day didn't make sense to Fred because it was late (9 p.m.) on Sunday night. It had been a long day. Fred was asleep even before the plane took off.

In the Land of Nod, he dreamed* that he was in the pet store again. This time he was sitting next to the parrot.

He explained to the parrot that he was going to Australia to teach mathematics.

The parrot told him, "I'm going to New York to teach feathers."

Fred's dreams could be really strange.

---

* The past tense of *dream* is *dreamed* or *dreamt.* Both are correct.

Most verbs have only one past tense. *Kneel* and *dream* are unusual.

look → looked — only one past tense
dance → danced — only one past tense
pull → pulled — only one past tense
teach → taught — only one past tense
ring → rang — only one past tense
tie → tied — only one past tense

> Time Out!
>
> In the footnote on the previous page was the sentence: **Most verbs have only one past tense.**
>
> Many readers might not know what a verb is.

small essay

What's a Verb?

Suppose I wrote a sentence with a bunch of persons, places, or things in it: Darlene bride dog Kansas car pizza.

What's wrong? There isn't any action in that sentence. The sentence doesn't have any verbs. Verbs tell you what is happening.

Darlene *smiles*. Brides *carry* flowers. Dogs *run* in Kansas. Cars *bring* pizzas.

Only verbs have past tenses. Darlene *smiled*. Brides *carried* flowers. Dogs *ran* in Kansas. Cars *brought* pizzas.

I love verbs. Without verbs the sun couldn't *shine*. My eyes couldn't *blink*. My brain couldn't *think*.

end of small essay

This sentence no verb.

Your Turn to Play

1. What is the past tense of these words?

    write

    look

    eat

2. Only verbs have past tenses. Why don't these words have past tenses?

    orange

    house

    Betty

3. Insert *that* or *which* in the blank.

    Verbs are words ______ have past tenses.

4. How many verbs are in this sentence?

    When the doorbell rang, Darlene ran to the door, opened it, saw that it was Joe, and gave him a big hug.

. . . . ANSWERS . . . .

1. write → wrote
   look → looked
   eat → ate
2. That's easy! They aren't verbs.
3. Verbs are words <u>that</u> have past tenses.

The phrase "that have past tenses" defines what kind of words we are talking about. It is essential to the meaning of the sentence. If you just wrote, "Verbs are words," the real meaning of the sentence would be lost.

Note the comma comes before the close-quotes.

4. There are six verbs.

When the doorbell rang, Darlene ran to the door, opened it, saw that it was Joe, and gave him a big hug.

All those six verbs are in the past tense.

The verb in the previous sentence is in the present tense.

Chapter Sixteen

Australia

The sun was shining in Fred's face. The flight attendant said, "Hey, wake up sleepy head."

Fred waved goodbye to the parrot in his dream and woke up.

All the other passengers had already deplaned. The plane had landed in Sydney, Australia. It was the day after Fred left Los Angeles. Fred had slept the whole trip.

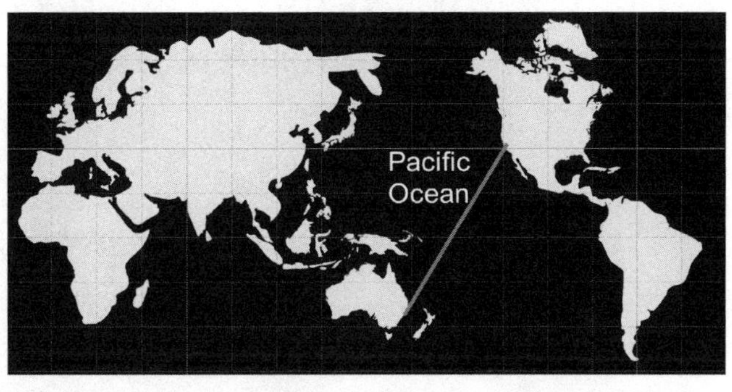

He was one of the few people in the world who had flown across the Pacific Ocean and never saw a drop of water.

It was June in Sydney. It was 59°F (or 15°C in the metric system). Winter was approaching.

Wait a minute! I, your reader, object. This is nuts. Everyone knows that's wrong. In June it is

getting warmer, not colder. You, Mr. Author, should have written that summer was approaching.

What "everyone knows" is sometimes wrong. Hundreds of years ago everyone knew that the earth was flat. That was obvious. It didn't look curved. If it were a ball, then people on the bottom side would fall off.

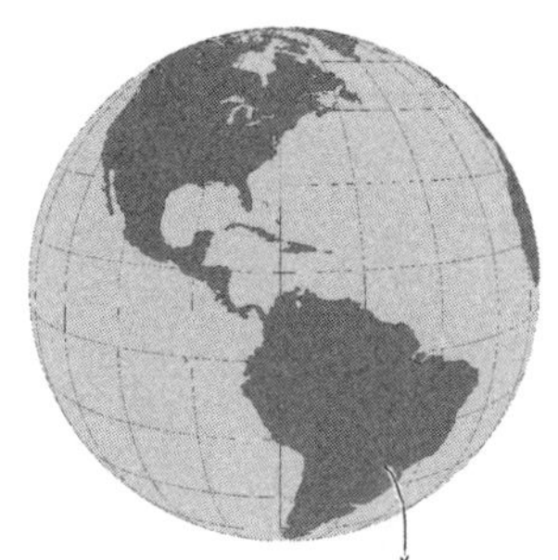

Some of the people who believed the earth was flat even misused the Bible to try to prove their "scientific" view of the earth.*

But what has this to do with winter in June?

I'm getting to that. Just because you like to sing Jingle Bells in December doesn't mean that the whole earth is the same as where you live.

The bottom half of the earth has its seasons reversed. Christmas comes in the warmer part of the year.

The equator is like a belt that goes around the tummy of the earth. Below (south) of the

---

* "[The Lord shall] gather together the dispersed of Judah from the four corners of the earth." Isaiah 11:12

equator it is warmest when it is coldest above (north) of the equator. If you don't believe me, you can look at the weather page in the newspaper each day for a year. The weather page often gives the temperature for different places on the earth.

World

City	Today Hi/Lo/W	City	Today Hi/Lo/W
Amsterdam	47/33/c	Montreal	70/43/sh
Athens	64/48/pc	Moscow	66/49/s
Auckland	70/57/sh	Nassau	83/73/pc
Baghdad	91/71/s	New Delhi	102/75/s
B. Aires	77/55/s	Oslo	50/32/c
Barbados	85/78/t	Paris	59/32/sh
Beijing	50/46/pc	Perth	77/52/c
Berlin	62/37/pc	Rio	79/68/pc
Bermuda	69/63/pc	Riyadh	99/75/s
Brussels	55/30/sh	Rome	65/54/s
Cairo	76/52/s	San Juan	80/73/t
Copenhagen	53/35/pc	Seoul	57/44/c
Dublin	53/36/c	Singapore	91/80/t
Frankfurt	58/39/sh	Stockholm	48/34/sh
Geneva	48/35/[illegible]	Sydney	68/55/sh
Guatemala City	81/63/t	Tel Aviv	70/53/sh
Helsinki	47/37/c	Tijuana	82/54/s
Hong Kong	79/70/t	Tokyo	57/45/c
Istanbul	58/47/pc	Toronto	59/37/sh
Jerusalem	63/46/pc	Vancouver	52/48/r
Johannesburg	64/48/t	Vienna	65/48/r
Lima	76/64/s	Warsaw	63/46/sh
Lisbon	74/56/s	Zurich	49/37/r
London	56/36/c		
Madrid	66/42/pc		
Manila	95/76/pc		
Melbourne	61/50/sh		
Mexico City	77/54/pc		
Monterrey	73/54/s		

Weather key: s-sunny, pc-partly cloudy, c-cloudy, sh-showers, t-thunderstorms, r-rain, sf-snow flurries, sn-snow, i-ice, w-windy, f-fog, na-not available

Today the high temperature in Sydney is 68°.*

Keep a record of the Sydney temperatures for a year. You will see that it gets warmer there when it gets colder in the United States or in Europe.

I just had a great thought.

Would you care to share it with me?

If I were super rich, I would live where I live now from the middle of spring until the middle of fall. Then I would move across the equator to my second house. There it would be the middle of spring. I would stay there until the middle of fall and then move back to my original house. I would get two summers (and no winters) each year.

You have learned a little geography, and it might have changed your life.**

---

* I cut this out of an April newspaper.

** That's what real education should do.

In mathematics a ball is called a sphere. In geography the half of the earth that is above the equator is called the Northern Hemisphere.

hemisphere = hemi + sphere

hemi comes from the Greek. It means "half."

semi comes from the Latin. It means "half."

hemi and *semi* are prefixes. A **prefix** attaches to the front part of a word and changes its meaning.

A sphere is a whole ball. A hemisphere is half of a ball.

Weekly means every seven days. Semiweekly means something that occurs twice a week. Semiannual means twice a year.

Some chocolate is marked "semisweet." That means that it is only half sweet. Adding more sugar would make it sweet.

Christina Rossetti is one of my favorite poets. In a poem called "May" she wrote:

With all sweet things it passed away
And left me old, and cold, and grey.

A line of poetry is called a **stich** (pronounced STICK).

With all sweet things it passed away is a stich.

Most college graduates don't know that *With all sweet things* is a hemistich.

Another hemistich is *it passed away*. A hemistich is a half line of poetry.

Your Turn to Play

1. *Annual* means once a year. Make a guess what semiannual means.

2. This is a circle. ○

Draw a picture of a semicircle.

3. *un* is a prefix that is used a lot: *unfed, unloved, unsung, unimportant, unlit, unmoved, unprepared, unrecognizable, unsaved, unsweetened, unable.*

The word *savory* means something that tastes good, smells good, or is pleasing and attractive. A savory meal can have all of these meanings.

Fill in the blank: A bowl of dirty water is a meal that you would call ___________. (Hint: Look at the previous two paragraphs.)

This is a paragraph. It starts with some white space at the beginning and continues on for one or more sentences.

This is a second paragraph. It is also indented (the white space).

This is a very short paragraph!

.......ANSWERS.......

1. *Semiannual* means something that happens twice a year. It happens every half year. It happens every six months.

2. Here are a bunch of semicircles.

3. A bowl of dirty water is a meal that you would call <u>unsavory</u>.

   The prefix *un* means "not."

Chapter Seventeen
Sydney

Fred was now in the Southern Hemisphere. It didn't feel much different than being in Kansas. No matter where you stand on the earth, it feels the same. If you drop a ball, it will fall toward your feet.

The Sydney airport was much smaller than the Los Angeles International Airport. Fred spotted a large sign that told him that his flight to Wagga Wagga would be leaving in an hour.

He sat down in the boarding area and waited for the announcement that it was time to board the plane.

Normally, Fred would have pulled out one of the books that he carried and spent the hour reading. But everything he had brought had gone with George on Old Smoker back to the repair shop and then had been mailed back to Fred's office. All he had with him was seven dollars.

Fred thought to himself *I'm waiting for Wagga Wagga.* He played with the words.

While we wait for Wagga Wagga.

A winter wait in Wagga Wagga.

Wind-whipped whistles in Wagga Wagga.

silent *t*

Fred was playing with **alliteration**,* using the same sound at the beginning of words.

Poets and advertisers often use alliteration.

Poetry: Rock-a-bye, baby
In the tree top,
When the wind blows,
The cradle will rock.
When the bough breaks,
The cradle will fall,
And down will come baby,
Cradle and all.

Advertising: Mealtime magic with milk.

Fred went a little alliteration crazy as he thought *Even without a watch I will not cause the Wagga Wagga men and women to wait for me. Wow. It's just June 3. I'm due the day after today.*

Fred saw a sign which said**:

The time is 2:40 p.m.

---

* a-litter-RAY-shun where *a* is like the *a* in alone.

** It is really hard to stop doing alliteration!

Then the sign changed.

Today is June 4

Fred rubbed his eyes. *I'm due at the Board of Missions office in Wagga Wagga on June 4!* he thought to himself. *I left Los Angeles on June 2. Flying across the Pacific Ocean doesn't take two days. It's got to be June 3.*

It is . . . in Los Angeles.

It is June 4 in Sydney.*

---

* This is not easy to explain. In this **footnote** is a super-quick explanation.

First, there are **time zones** around the world. If it is 2:40 p.m. where you are right now, then it is now 1:40 p.m. for someone who is roughly 700–1,000 miles to the west of you. It is 3:40 p.m. for someone who is roughly 700–1,000 to the east of you. There are 24 times zones around the world. There are pictures and more explanation of time zones in Chapter 3 of *Life of Fred: Honey.*

Second, there is the **International Date Line** out in the middle of the Pacific Ocean. When you cross it heading west, you suddenly advance a day on the calendar. In the middle of Fred's flight, when he was asleep, June 3 suddenly became June 4. More explanation is in Chapter 15 of *Life of Fred: Edgewood.* Both of these Fred books are in the math series.

Fred pulled Jennifer's letter out of his pocket and read the last paragraph:

> If interested, please let us know and report to our office in Wagga Wagga on June 4.

Fred thought to himself *It's 2:40 right now. The plane to Wagga Wagga will be leaving in an hour. That's 3:40. It's going to be after four o'clock when we get to Wagga Wagga. And then I have to find the Board of Missions office before it closes.*

Fred was in a panic. *Will I lose my math teaching job if I show up late? Will they give the job to someone else? How late does the office stay open?*

The time from 2:40 to 3:40 went by very slowly. 2:40 → 2:41 → 2:42 → 2:43 → 2:44 → 2:45 → 2:46 → 2:47 → 2:48 → 2:49 → 2:50 → 2:51 → 2:52 → 2:53 → 2:54 → 2:55 → 2:56 → 2:57 → 2:58 → 2:59 → 3:00 → 3:01 → 3:02 → 3:03 → 3:04 → 3:05 → 3:06 → 3:07 → 3:08 → 3:09 → 3:10 → 3:11 → 3:12 → 3:13 → 3:14 → 3:15 → 3:16 → 3:17 → 3:18 → 3:19 → 3:20 → 3:21 → 3:22 → 3:23 → 3:24 → 3:25 → 3:26 → 3:27 → 3:28 → 3:29 → 3:30 → 3:31 → 3:32 → 3:33 → 3:34 → 3:35 → 3:36 → 3:37 → 3:38 → 3:39 → 3:40

The sign on the wall said

The time is 3:40 p.m.

That was the longest hour of Fred's life.

At 3:44 boarding of the plane began.

An extra four minutes! Fred thought. He didn't realize that planes, trains, and buses often run late.

Your Turn to Play

1. In Chapter 4, we learned four different ways to make plurals.

❶ add an *s* one dog → two dogs
❷ *f* becomes *ves* one shelf → two shelves
❸ crazy changes one goose → two geese
❹ no change one fish → two fish

If you look at the sentence just before this Your Turn to Play, find a fifth way to make plurals.

2. Circle alliteration in this famous poem.

Little Boy Blue
Come blow your horn,
The sheep's in the meadow,
The cow's in the corn.

.......ANSWERS.......

1. bus → buses
   dress → dresses
   caress → caresses   caress = a loving touch
   success → successes

❺ If the word ends in *s*, add *es*.

2. Little Boy Blue
   Come blow your horn,
   The sheep's in the meadow,
   The cow's in the corn.

Two Uses of the Apostrophe

1. To show ownership.

   Joe's jellybeans

   Fred's doll

   the sheep's hat 

2. To indicate something is left out.

The cow's in the corn. → The cow is in the corn.

He can't → He cannot

There are five ways we have learned to make things plural. None of those ways uses an apostrophe.

Chapter Eighteen
In a Hurry

Fred ran onto the plane. He found his seat in a hurry. He buckled his seat belt. He sat up straight. In short, he did everything he could to make the plane take off as quickly as possible.

All the other passengers walked. They chatted with their friends as they found their seats.

It was ten minutes to four. The flight attendant stood up and showed everyone how to put on a seat belt. That took another two minutes. Fred wanted to point to his seat belt to show that he already had his on—anything to hurry things up.

3:50

Finally, the plane taxied* to the runway and took off. It had been a long trip: the bus ride to Wichita, the flight to Los Angeles, the flight to Sydney, and now the flight to Wagga Wagga.

After takeoff the flight attendant stood up again and said, "This flight will be a very short one."

---

* Airplanes taxi on the ground and fly in the air.

Fred thought *Yes! Yes! Yes!*

She continued, "Therefore, we will not be serving peanuts and soft drinks."

Fred thought *I'm really not hungry right now. I just want to get there before the Board of Missions office closes.*

She said, "For those of you who are new to Wagga Wagga, here is an information sheet." She passed out the sheets.

At first, Fred didn't want to read it because that would take time. Then he realized that not reading it wouldn't make the plane go any faster.

alliteration

Welcome to Wagga Wagga

photo credit: Bidgee

The Wiradjuri people were the first people to inhabit this region. In their language *Wagga* meant crow.

The Wiradjuri didn't make their words plural by adding an *s*.* They were much more logical. To make a word plural, they just repeated the word twice. *Wagga* meant crow, and *Wagga Wagga* meant crows.

Instead of saying, "How many sisters do you have?" you would say, "How many sister sister do you have?"

Fred giggled. He thought of the word *autobiography* (auto-bye-OG-graf-ee). That's a story you write about your life.

He pictured going into a library and asking the librarian, "Where are the autobiography autobiography located?"

It would be much easier to ask, "Where are the autobiographies located?"

Wait! I, your reader, just noticed something. Do you realize what you, Mr. Author, just did?

What do you mean? I didn't do anything.

---

* Or by any of the other ways we make plurals in English. The plural of *mouse* is *mice*, but the plural of *house* is not *hice*.

Yes, you did. You snuck* in a new way to make a plural.

You mean *autobiography autobiography*?

No, silly. I mean autobiographies.

story → stories

berry → berries

body → bodies

city → cities

enemy → enemies

That means there are SIX ways to make plurals in English! If it ends in y, change it to ies.

You are almost right. You have forgotten about boy → boys, monkey → monkeys, and bay → bays. The official rule is *y* becomes *ies*, unless the letter before the *y* is a **vowel** (*a*, *e*, *i*, *o*, or *u*).

The flight attendant said, "Please make sure your seat is in its upright and locked position and your seat belt is fastened. We are about to land."

Fred could think of no happier words.

---

* The past tense of sneak can be either *sneaked* or *snuck*. Both are correct. The main thing to remember is to stay consistent. If you use *sneaked* in one paragraph, don't switch to *snuck* in the next paragraph. That would drive your readers crazy.

Your Turn to Play

1. Make the plural of each of these six words. (These six words use the six different ways of making a plural in English.)

eighty

business

head

foot

deer (Hint: It's the same as sheep.)

wolf

2. What is the past tense of these verbs?

sing

bark

slide

3. Circle the alliteration in the first two lines of this famous poem.

Ring around the rosey,
A pocket full of posies.

. . . . ANSWERS . . . .

1. eighty → eighties (The temperature will be in the eighties today.)
   business → businesses (She started three businesses.)
   head → heads
   foot → feet
   deer → deer (I saw three deer in the forest.)
   wolf → wolves

2. Yesterday I sang in the choir.
   Last night the dog barked for an hour.
   He slid into third base.

3. Ring around the rosey,
   A pocket full of posies.

Of course, there is a seventh way to make plurals in English.

No! No! You can't do this to me. I, your reader, want a simpler language, like that of the Wiradjuri.

Of course, there will be fewer books and fewer films in that language.

Okay. Let's get it over with.

The seventh way is pretty rare. Latin-based words ending in *us*. A male graduate of a school is called an alumnus. Male graduates are alumni.

The eighth way is even rarer. A female graduate is called an alumna. Female graduates are alumnae.

Chapter Nineteen
Wagga Wagga

It was half past four. Fred deplaned. He saw the sign that read **Wagga Wagga Airport**, but he couldn't see the city.

He wondered *How am I going to find the Board of Missions office when I can't even find the city?*

He turned to an airline employee and asked alliteratively, "Where's Wagga Wagga?"

She smiled and pointed northwest. "Wagga is seven miles* in that direction. We don't put airports in the middle of cities."

Fred asked, "Why only one Wagga?" (Words that are alliterative do not have to start with the same letter. They have to start with the same sound.)

He didn't realize that many Australians shorten their double-named towns to a single name. Woy Woy is often called Woy by Australians.

Over the airport loudspeakers came the silly song by the country music artists Greg

---

* Actually, she said 11 kilometers. The whole world uses the metric system (kilometers, kilograms, liters) except for one major country: the U.S.A.

Champion and Jim Hayes, *Don't call Wagga Wagga Wagga.*" (a real song by real people)

The song wasn't very popular in other countries because only Australians knew what the song was about.

Then Fred suddenly realized that he didn't know where in Wagga Wagga was the Board of Missions office.

He opened the letter and looked at the last paragraph:

> If interested, please let us know and report to our office in Wagga Wagga on June 4.
>
> Sincerely,
>
> *Jennifer Glory*
>
> Jennifer Glory
> Board chairman

The letter didn't tell him!

What Had Happened

After Fred had sent his *"Dear Jennifer, Yes!"* letter, he had spent five minutes packing his clothes. Then he packed his pencils, paper, clipboards and lots of math books. That took another two minutes.

In seven minutes he was out of the office and heading toward the bus station. Not many people can pack for a summer's adventure that quickly.

After Jennifer had received Fred's "*Yes!*" letter, she wrote him a long letter describing

❀ how happy she was that he was coming,

❀ how to get to the Wagga Wagga office, and

❀ what classes he would be teaching.

The letter arrived three minutes after Fred left.

When Kingie got the letter, he didn't know what to do with it. He had no idea where Fred was going. He wrote on the envelope, "***Fred has left. Unable to forward this. Please return to sender.***" Kingie has very good handwriting.

Jennifer knew exactly what to do. She wrote to the people at the Wagga Wagga office.

They celebrated that Fred was coming.

They found out what plane Fred would be on and sent Mack to greet him at the airport. Mack didn't know what Fred looked like. He had just been told to look for someone who was a college professor named Fred.

Mack waits for Fred

Mack found a good spot to wait.

He waited.

He saw people who were obviously tourists. He saw families with six kids. He saw a pair of women. He saw a man in an army uniform. He saw a little boy with a square head. He saw an airline pilot.

But he didn't see anyone who looked like a college professor. Mack climbed down and wandered through (silent o, g, and h) the crowd. He thought (silent u, g, and h) of making a sign (silent g) that read, "I'm looking for a college professor named Fred." He could hold the sign up high (silent g and h) and he hoped that Fred would see it. But he didn't have anything with which to make a sign.

Fred and Mack were standing right next to each other. Fred was looking for a bus or a taxi so that he could get to Wagga Wagga. Mack was looking for Fred.

Life can sometimes be very silly.

Mack headed back to his car. There hadn't been that many passengers on the plane, and none of them could have been a college professor.

Fred noticed Mack's car.

Fred couldn't believe his eyes. He ran up to Mack and said, "I have to get to the Board of Missions office today. Are you going there?"

Mack laughed and said, "Yes, I am. After I find a college professor named Fred."

Fred smiled.

Index

See the footnote on page 86 of this book.